STORIES OF A
WEST VIRGINIA DOCTOR'S
SON

Greenbrier Almond, MD

Greenbrier Almond, MD

2012

International Standard Book Number 0-87012-821-3
Library of Congress Control Number 2012914607
Printed in the United States of America
Copyright © 2012 by Greenbrier Almond
Buckhannon, WV
All Rights Reserved
2012

McClain Printing Company
Parsons, WV
www.mcclainprinting.com
2012

Cover photos by Lois Flanagan Almond

Illustrations by Noel W. Tenney

DEDICATION

Dedicated to our granddaughters Aliza Eloise Almond Pope and Harper Rose Landin Almond. Growing up as a child of Appalachia has been a joy that I wish to convey, with the prayer that this next generation of our family will have tender loving care memories of home, family, community, and nature.

Illustrator Noel W. Tenney is a native of Upshur County, WV where he lives and maintains his Old Orchard Studio. He has been an educator for more than forty years and has taught in public schools and higher education. He currently serves as Cultural Specialist and faculty for the Gabor WV Folklife Center on the campus of Fairmont State University and Pierpont Community and Technical College in Fairmont, WV, and as Director of Special Projects for the Upshur County Historical Society. His art work addresses a "sense of place" of the West Virginia landscape and environment.

TABLE OF CONTENTS

FOREWORD

Stories of a West Virginia Doctor's Son is not just a treasure of memories; it is a portrait of family love. Children are immersed in a wealth of experiences, filled with fun and laughter, while parents capture teachable moments for history, geography, and science. Perhaps more importantly, the memories relayed by Dr. Almond reflect the high regard his parents placed on the need for aspirations, goals, and high moral values. Appreciation for truth, justice, and respect for all, regardless of their walk of life, were qualities instilled by loving parents.

It is attributes such as these that parents, teachers, and all who serve as role models can instill in children's lives through their daily walk with them. Through his eyes, the author has given the reader a look into the beauty of a family life built on a foundation with love, compassion, learning, and trust as the cornerstones.

Truly these are beautiful memories worth reading and lessons of life to treasure and share.

Helen G. Reger

Helen G. Reger taught West Virginia's first public kindergarten class in 1958. She spent many years teaching in Upshur County, earning the West Virginia Teacher of the Year award in 1976.

ACKNOWLEDGMENTS

I offer a special thanks to my sisters K, Anne, Ruthie, and Beth, with whom I lived these childhood stories. We have shared memories that are rich and fruitful and fun.

Kimberly Gilmore has been a compassionate and yet very competent editor. Rarely have I shared partially composed thoughts with anyone. She has guided the creative process well. A special thanks goes to her.

Araceli, my wife of nearly 37 years and the Lola to our grandchildren, has heard the telling and retelling of these stories, sometimes in the middle of the night, and sometimes on a long walk in the woods. As I am Lolo and she is Lola to Aliza and Harper Rose, I wanted her wisdom and spiritual discernment in each and every story.

Of course, without Maria and Justin as well as Yasmine and Ronce, there would be no grandchildren inspiring the telling of these tales. Thank you.

Finally, *inspired* means "God-breathed," as well as breathing into the lungs physiologically. From the very moment that I learned of the pregnancies of Maria and Yasmine, I felt the creative urge to write these stories of childhood, believing God would give us grandchildren who would share our air, our lives, and our joy.

INTRODUCTION

As a little boy, I had a fascination with my father's shoes. I have an early memory of slipping my too-small feet into Daddy's shoes. I clip-clopped from the bedroom toward the kitchen. As I clomped into the kitchen, Mom looked up from her cooking and exclaimed, "Oh Greenbrier, it is you! I thought you were Dad. You sound just like him." I beamed with glee. Truly, I wanted to be just like him. The stories that follow come from my heart. I could not have had better parents. I could not have chosen to follow a better man.

"Always exceed your patient's expectations!" my father declared during a live broadcast of my weekly television program, *Tender Loving Care*, streaming out through our local community access television channel. Doc was responding to my query about the art of medicine. I had followed my father, Harold D. Almond, MD, into the practice of medicine, but I had yet to have my patients love me like his loved him.

"Dad," I said exasperated, "that is a prescription for burnout." Even West Virginia University Medical School Dean, Robert D'Alessandri, MD, praised Doc on the opening day of class in 1998, when he invited Dad to tell three stories from his memoir, *The Stories of a West Virginia Doctor*.

Dean "Bob" explained, "You will learn much about the scientific basis of medicine in the next four years, but today you will learn much about the compassion and caring of our healing profession." The students appeared impressed and came forward for autographs afterward.

Doc stuck by his guns on the television show as he recalled his brother's death from erysipelas when he himself was ten years old. There were no antibiotics, and witch hazel did not cure. Doc prayed to God for a chance to be a physician. God heard his prayer, though much happened along the way, including his mother's death, the Great Depression, and World War II. "I wanted my chance to practice medicine and I got it!"

Still pondering Dad's remarks the next evening, I covered the office while he delivered a baby at St. Joseph's Hospital. A mother with three coughing and wheezing children came in and waited. Doc worked without appointments. "I want to see folk when they are sick. If they have to wait two weeks for an appointment, they will either be well or be dead." After examining the children and prescribing medication, I told Mom that it would be $10.00 for each child, as this was Doc's customary fee. She acted surprised. "No," she insisted, "when I bring all three at the same time, Doc only charges for one." I replied, "Yes, of course, that will be $10.00. You are fortunate to have such fine children."

My memory of trying on Daddy Doc's shoes leads me to a tender concern for the next generation of children who will grow into adulthood. Whose "shoes" will they wear? I feel impelled to tell the grandchildren of my upbringing. I do not want them to wander down a dead-end path in life. Perhaps something I say will help them grow in wisdom.

We have a lifetime of stories to tell to one another and to our grandchildren!!! Stories teach lessons not only about practicing medicine but also about practicing family. Lois Flanagan Almond gave me a short course on life when she offered up her last earthly words to me:

* Have fun
* Encourage children
* Introduce Jesus to people and people to Jesus.

Mom, I've done my best.

****

The stories that follow are my recollections. Certainly my boyhood is from a different time and place than my grandchildren will experience. Hopefully by telling these tales, along with some emphasis on lessons learned, I will help prepare the next generation for an abundant life.

> What are little girls made of?
> What are little boys made of?

Perhaps the sweetest moment at the end of a long spring season of childhood and youth occurred after I was already in college. Stanley Martin, West Virginia Wesleyan College President, came to our little "alma mater of the mountains" in the late 1950s to fully develop a beautiful campus and the physical plant. He wished for the college students to be competent, cultured, and Christian. In the middle of the campus, he built the the largest chapel in West Virginia. He asked me to represent the youth of West Virginia at the cornerstone laying. What a high privilege! What a wonderful rite of passage from my own childhood to my early manhood! The granite marker has the bold statement of John Wesley:

> "Best of all, God is with us."

Greenbrier Almond, MD
01 June 2012

©Noel W. Tenney 97

STRAWBERRY LAND
BUCKHANNON, WEST VIRGINIA

FAMILY LIFE

NEW BEGINNINGS

We always had a collie dog, and his name was always Brier. My Brier, however, acted more like a sheepdog. He loved me and would herd me around the small yard at Cabin #5 along the railroad track in Gibbon, Nebraska, where I lived my first two years.

Dad was serving in the Army Air Corps, including most of a year spent in Japan, so he missed being with us when my sister K was born. I'm sure Mom was lonely for him, but she had her girlfriends who had similar military wives' tales of woe. Early pictures of Brier and me show us having a lot of fun. But when Dad returned from Japan, and it was time to go back to West Virginia, we decided Brier should go back to sheep herding. We took him out to a farm, where he hesitated to leave my side. But I ordered him to chase the sheep, and he did. He looked back to see if I meant it, and I waved him on. My parents later said that we both took it pretty well.

Being born in Nebraska earned K and me the nickname of "Nebraska Rascals" from Mom and Dad. I left a piece of my heart there in Nebraska when I left Brier, but I did not look back when we headed for West Virginia to become mountaineers. Maybe, however, I should have looked back at least one time.

Mom and Dad would shake their heads in disbelief, with a twinkle in their eyes, whenever they would tell of what I did on the way to our new home. We drove with all our earthly belongings piled high on our 1938 Chevrolet. Two kids in diapers and a young couple in love, feeling free from World War II and Northwestern University School of Medicine, headed for the hills of home. What a sight. But with a son named Greenbrier and a "Nebraska Rascal" at that, all cannot be calm and peaceful for long.

As the tale is told, I played with a baby powder can, probably trying to open it and powder my sister K. In a moment of glee, I threw the can of powder up in the air. The wind caught it and out the window it flew. The car behind us became a bullseye which I hit. Lo and behold, the canister exploded, sending powder liberally over the windshield and greatly surprising the driver.

Probably like many folks after a long and hard-fought war, he was easily spooked. He sped up and started yelling at Dad. Finally he passed our overloaded vehicle and drove us off the road to confront Dad. How surprised he was when he realized that the powder was not a bomb. And furthermore, the culprit was a mere lad named Greenbrier, who earned his nickname that day as a "Nebraska Rascal."

ZIP-A-DEE-DOO-DAH

Memories of our routine of bedtime and a Brer Rabbit story from Dad stay embedded in my heart to this day. Being the oldest of five had a definite advantage when it came to story time; I had extra doses. Maybe because Joel Chandler Harris was red headed and Daddy Doc was red headed. Maybe because our rough-riding President, Teddy Roosevelt, said, "Presidents come and Presidents go, but Uncle Remus stays put." Whatever the reason, Dad loved to tell us Brer Rabbit stories.

What fun to hurry through our bath and get set for Dad's story. They were serialized as a running tale. Brer Rabbit had to outsmart Brer Fox every night. Sometimes a friendly but slow Brer Terrapin entered the story line. Seasonally, and perhaps after we visited the French Creek Game Farm, Brer Bear would lumber through the storyline.

Dad focused a great deal on the haven of the brier patch as the home for the rabbits. Of course with a name like Greenbrier, the thick brier patch often made it into my dreams as a safe place to be. Dad did not attempt to mimic the dialects in the stories, preferring instead to tell them in his own voice. However, he did have phrases like "elevenity-eleven," meaning a long time, that made it into our household usage.

Dad would begin the tale after Mom led us in prayers. She would have us kneel at the bedside. That quieted us a bit. Then we would gather in Mom and Dad's bed with the warm blankets covering us. The lights would be turned down. Dad would lie down across the bottom of bed and wonder pensively, "Where were we last night?"

K, who tracked the stories the best of us all, would remind Dad, "Brer Rabbit, hopping along, yelled out to Brer Fox, 'You will never capture me now. For I was born and bred in a brier patch!'" Dad would wink at me at that point. I'd giggle.

At this point, Annie would plead for a retelling of the details of her own birth. This might lead Dad down a side trail to tell of the legendary snowstorm of 1950, with 4 feet of snow and the Thanksgiving holiday of Annie's birth. Of course, Brer Bear would be hibernating and warm.

Ruthie would show interest in Brer Rabbit's bungalow house down under the ground. In particular she would wonder about the kitchen. Of course, Dad would embellish the tale, making sure there was a fireplace with smoke coming out of the chimney. Brer Rabbit loved to eat his carrots, he would remind us. We all knew we could see better at night if we ate carrots.

Bethie, bless her heart, missed the earlier stories, but she joined us when I was ten years old. She loved to hear about Brer Terrapin. Aesop's Fables and Brer Rabbit sometimes got mixed up at this point, as Dad may tell of the Hare and the Tortoise, reminding us that the race of life is won by the one who keeps on running, not necessarily by the fastest runner.

Sleep came quickly. Dad carefully carried us to our separate beds, tucking us in. He would rub his cheek against mine so that I could feel his rough whiskers. Then he'd ask playfully if he had Brer Rabbit whiskers. In dreamland, I'd imagine myself hopping over the hills, twirling my long whiskers and singing at the top of my voice, "Zip-a-dee-doo-dah!"

THE BIG TEASE

What a birthday present for my 13th birthday, when a blizzard hits central West Virginia and school is closed! Mom promises a steak dinner, and Martha Daniel, my best friend Danny's mother, bakes a lamb-shaped cake, chocolate inside and green icing for the grass and white icing for the lamb. A party is planned with neighbors dropping by. We will play some Ping-Pong and maybe Monopoly.

My four sisters have hinted at my presents. Dad and Mom indicate that Boy Scout camping and cooking equipment, on my wish list, will be my big gift.

Nobody is teasing me with the nursery rhyme that can make me hopping mad or bring tears, the one about little boys being made of "snips and snails and puppy dog tails," while also saying that little girls are made of "sugar and spice and everything nice." A really good day is shaping up.

Mom sends us to the basement to play, as we are pretty wild after sleigh riding down the backyard hill to our heart's content (and to the limit of how much cold our feet and hands could stand). Her hot chocolate warms us up but also revs us up.

No excuses though. I take Ruthie's red bike and am riding it around the chimney, furnace, and the Ping-Pong table. Ruthie, of course, wants her bike for her own riding. "No way!" I tease her. I begin to speed away from her as she shrieks and runs after me.

Faster and faster I ride. Bike riding indoors probably should have a very slow speed limit if one thinks about it. But hey! I am now a teenager. School is not in session. Who is thinking?

The last thing I remember is sliding around the cider press, leaning into a tight curve and slamming into the rock polishing equipment. Like Dad has taught us, when you crash, check for broken bones. My left leg is definitely broken.

Dad takes me to the hospital for x-rays. The fibula is cracked. I'll be six weeks in a walking cast. The good news is that all my friends can sign their names on the plaster of Paris cast. The bad news is that I have my toes exposed to the cold winter, since Dad has to monitor the health of my skin and circulation down to the tips of my toes.

The birthday party is pretty subdued. The "Big Tease" got his comeuppance!!!

ROCK HOUND

Fantasy versus reality has always fascinated me, clear back to the Academy Grade School carnivals. The classroom of my third-grade teacher, Miss Swisher, looked mysterious and utterly transformed by lamps covered with colored shawls and crepe paper hanging down, lowering the ceiling. In the middle of the room was a turbaned man sitting in front of a crystal ball. Even his face was partly draped, but I could see his dancing eyes as I paid my dime and took my seat on a cushion. The fortune teller told me to show him my open palms as he placed his large hands under mine. His voice sounded like West Virginia Wesleyan College Professor George Rossbach's, but he did not look at all like him tonight. Of course this was all for fun, but they put on quite a show.

Again his large hands began to move back and forth over the crystal ball, and mist arose from under the coffee table, also covered with a scarf of bright colors. He began to speak slowly and mysteriously. "I see your future," he observed. Suddenly I was frightened. "Don't worry," he instructed. "The future looks great. I see rocks of many sizes and many colors. I see diamonds. Look—emeralds. Much gold. Even pearls."

Wow! Now I was excited. I'd have to tell my great-uncle Paul, who was a rock hound. That is what Mom and Dad called him. I thanked the wizard for my fortune, relieved and excited.

Uncle Paul always seemed a gruff man to me, and he smelled of garlic and sweat. But the next day I was not afraid of him. He was pleased by my fortune and demonstrated it by showing me his agates and fool's gold. We put brown sugar in his tumbler and polished more stones, preparing Christmas gifts of earrings and tie pins.

Even Grandmother Mary, Uncle Paul's sister, appeared pleased at my fortune. She said that rocks grew in her

8

garden. She needed help getting the rocks out of the soil to make room for her pansies. After school I helped her build a rock wall with stones we dug out. Sometimes Grandfather Paul Flanagan, Grandmother Mary Flanagan, Uncle Paul Barnes, and our entire family would drive out to Audra Park to swim in the Middle Fork of the Tygart River. There we would gather round, smooth rocks for decorating the edges of the flower beds.

Dad sounded overjoyed that rocks were in my future. He hatched a plan for visiting all "Seven Natural Wonders of Upshur County," including a natural bridge near Carter, where a stream flowed under a large rock and one drove on the road over the same rock.

Mom liked the idea, too. She told Dad it was time for us to climb the tallest rock pile in West Virginia. The Spruce Knob hike became our Christmas picture snapshot that year. We packed our picnic basket in the morning, loaded up our green Jeep, and headed for the tallest mountain in West Virginia. Spruce Knob was shy of one mile high, so enterprising West Virginia mountaineers stacked loose rock up to elevate the peak. We added the Almond rocks to the heap.

Years later I'd fall in love with Araceli, who hailed from the "Pearl of the Pacific," the mountaintop islands of the Philippines. They jut upward from the deepest trenches of the Pacific Ocean to form 7,200 islands strung like a necklace of pearls across the mighty sea. We love our little Tablas Island with its steep volcanic rock peak and central caldera.

And many moons later, Araceli and I planted our own flowers in our own rock garden in the side yard of our dear home, at the side of a pleasant street that the Indians named "white rock," or in their language, "Kanawha."

How fortune has smiled on me.

9

PLAYING THE GAME

Life is not about winning or losing. Life is about how you play the game. I want my grandchildren to know this lesson. Here is how I learned it from the school of hard knocks.

Mom had older half-brothers and half-sisters. The Flanagans lived through hard times, doing the best they could. My Uncle Kester joined the Navy and saw the world. He had been everywhere. He could do anything. When my grandparents retired from ministry with the Methodist Church, Uncle Kester showed up and helped build a wonderful little brick cottage at the bottom of our hill. This was their first house after 50 years of itinerant ministry. Uncle Kester would be in our family slideshow pictures we projected on the wall, but he became a cause for laughter. Our joke began when I pointed to his picture on the wall the very moment Mom removed the slide. Of course, I was left pointing at a blank wall. How we laughed. Thanks, Uncle Kester, for adapting to whatever life brought your way. Thanks for being part of the family. Thanks for being the brunt of a good joke. A blank wall has become cause for the remark, "There's Uncle Kester!"

One of Uncle Kester's moves involved auctioning off his General Store up "Dirty Holler" in Calhoun County, West Virginia. Our family received his Ping-Pong table. What a prize. Mom and Dad taught us all to serve and to return and to play fairly our games of 21 points. But, as the saying goes, the rest is history. We grew up a tight-knit group on the hill. The older kids played well with the younger kids. Our basement with the Ping-Pong table became the center of winter activity. That little Ping-Pong ball can be given a down spin, up spin, curving spin to the left, curving spin to the right, and, of course, it can be slammed for dramatic points earned.

We become excellent Ping-Pong players. Buckhannon-

Upshur High School has a yearly intramural Ping-Pong tournament. In turn, Danny Morgan wins, then Billy Morgan, then Danny Daniels, followed by Bill Shissler. Finally, my turn. But lo and behold, I lose in the final Ping-Pong championship round to Laura TerlaakPoot. I break up a hilltop dynasty by losing to a girl. My, my. However, Uncle Kester's lesson of life saves my day. Life is not about winning or losing. Life is about how you play the game. Just to show Laura that I am a gracious loser, I ask her out to our junior-senior prom. She says "thanks but no thanks" and goes with my good friend Brent Reed. Uncle Kester, I needed another lesson from you about winning and losing at life.

RAINBOWS

I set My rainbow in the cloud, and it shall be for the sign of the covenant between Me and the earth. It shall be, when I bring a cloud over the earth, that the rainbow shall be seen in the cloud; and I will remember My covenant which is between Me and you and every living creature of all flesh; the waters shall never again become a flood to destroy all flesh. The rainbow shall be in the cloud, and I will look on it to remember the everlasting covenant between God and every living creature of all flesh that is on the earth.

-Genesis 9:13-16 (King James Version)

Dad and Mom both loved rainbows.

Was it a spiritual love? Yes, in part, for they treasured their roots at West Virginia Wesleyan College. Hiking the hills around Buckhannon during their courtship included viewing rainbows. The promise of God in a bow is an exciting story that I heard many times growing up.

Was it a scientific love? Yes, in part, as they both loved biology, the life science. Dad taught me the mnemonic "Roy G. Biv" for the colors of the rainbow: red, orange, yellow, green, blue, indigo, violet. Mom experienced what is generally called a near-death experience near the end of her life while at the West Virginia University Medical Center undergoing aortic valve replacement. When she came back to her body from her heavenly encounter, she exclaimed in wonder, "The colors are out of this world!!!"

Was it a cultural love? Yes, in part, as Dad's Scottish heritage and Mom's Irish heritage both expressed good luck and a pot of gold at the end of the rainbow.

Was it a romantic love? Yes, indeed. "I will" meant a promise for life. How romantic Mom and Dad became when they recalled looking at a rainbow from Twin Rock Hill overlooking Buckhannon, spying the pot of gold at the site that they later bought for $1,500. On that site they built their dream home for a low interest loan charging $48 interest the first month, $47 interest the second month, $46 interest the third month, and so on.

Rainbows in the basic meaning are simply arcs of colored light resulting from light rays and moisture, but for my parents, rainbows meant so much more.

Expecting grandchildren, I posted an announcement on Facebook: "Children are the rainbows of life. Grandchildren are the pots of gold at the end of the rainbows."

IT AIN'T OVER. . .

Memoir writing definitely has benefits. My father Doc writing about his practice of medicine set a standard for me. Having grandchildren has inspired my effort to recall memories.

What memory could be better than the time Great-Uncle Edward Barnes invited Dad and me to come to Cincinnati, Ohio to see the Reds and the New York Yankees in the 1961 World Series of Major League Baseball? In batting practice before the game, the "Bronx Bombers," Roger Maris and Mickey Mantle, hit many long balls to center field where we sat in the hot fall sun. Like those around us, I scrambled for a ball. Later on, Roger Maris signed his ball. This was the year he beat Babe Ruth's home run record of 60 home runs set in 1927. Dad told me that Babe was still champ because the American League had increased their game number by eight, as they added two expansion teams. Dad recalled going across the Hudson River from Maplewood, New Jersey to New York City to see the Yankees play in "The House That Ruth Built." Pitcher Whitey Ford was winning his second World Series Game of this World Series and pitching 14 shutout innings. In fact, he was on a roll from the regular season, pitching 32 scoreless innings and besting Babe Ruth, who had pitched 29⅔ such innings. Whitey became the most valuable player.

Great-Uncle Edward, my Grandmother Flanagan's younger brother, proved a perfect host. Great-Aunt Mary and he welcomed us to their modest brick home where we enjoyed World Series hot dogs. For dessert we had Keebler Cookies, since his trucking firm delivered them from Philadelphia to Cincinnati and all points in between. His passion was for photography, so he recorded our adventure and showed us albums of memories from the Barnes family.

The Barnes, being lifelong Methodists, also worked at the Methodist Publishing House in Cincinnati, so they gave us a tour through this massive operation. Dad wrote as a feature reporter for the *Buckhannon Record* many human interest stories about the unique folk living in our mountain community. On this trip, away from the bustle of medical practice, Dad was in great form as a storyteller. As a family, we laughed until we cried at his tales.

The ballgame was almost anticlimactic, the fifth and final game of the Series. But as New York Yankees catcher Yogi Berra said, "It ain't over 'til it's over." For me, it ain't over, thanks to the memories.

THE BARRISTER'S BOOKCASE
AND
THE TRAVELER'S WOODEN TRUNK

"Pick yourself up and dust yourself off," Grandmother Flanagan counseled. "Your Grandfather, the Reverend Paul L. Flanagan, and I did this many times in the itinerate ministry with the Methodist Church," she elaborated. She tended to call him by his titled name out of respect. My mother felt that they worked as co-pastors. Even with teamwork, the Flanagans came up against some pretty impossible situations. Grandmother wanted me to understand. To make her point, she asked me to come to her bedroom so she could show me a secret. "David," she said, using the the name she preferred to call me in solemn moments, "I want you to learn our secret of survival."

As we walked down the short hallway, she pointed out a barrister's bookcase at the end of the hall. "For 50 years we only owned two things: that bookcase and our traveler's wooden trunk. In the itinerate ministry that God called us to, we packed little, owned nothing but our books, and traveled much." We entered her bedroom, and she asked me to scoot the trunk out from under the bed. I lifted it onto the bed as she requested. Grandmother found her key and unlatched the simple wooden case. She felt around the bottom among carefully folded linen cloth. She pulled out a letter even as she began to weep. Rubbing the tears away, she handed the note to me and asked me to read it.

The paper was yellow and the crease in the fold was cracked. Upon opening it, I could see that it was a letter directed to my grandparents by one of their church's Pastor-Parish Relations Committees. The years of service noted. The church building noted. The membership rolls increasing noted. The radio ministry, *Stay on the Sunny Side*, broadcast across the nation, laudatory. However, the children were rowdy and unseemly for a pastor's kids, requiring a change in ministry.

Grandmother had an itinerate ministry of her own prior to her marriage to Reverend Flanagan. After his wife died, leaving him with four sons and two daughters, he sought a strong helpmeet. She prayerfully considered marriage and instant motherhood, knowing there would be monumental challenges. As a deaconess in the Methodist Church, she had met other tasks head-on, such as offering traveler's aid to young female immigrants coming to America, arriving through Union Station in Washington, DC. She kept her eyes peeled for young females wandering the train station, and approached them with a smile and a promise of a meal and shelter. Later on she met the challenge of helping young women who might be led astray on Wheeling Island in the Ohio River. Her goal was to rescue them from a life of prostitution. When she met Reverend Flanagan, she was serving as a midwife and spiritual mentor to women in the hardwood capital of the world—Richwood, West Virginia. Grandmother knew how to bring peace to the rough and tumble side of life. Serving as stepmother to six children, along with being the pastor's wife, was yet another challenge Grandmother met with grace. Always able, she mastered her life lessons.

"What did your Grandfather and I do? We picked ourselves up and we dusted ourselves off, just like Jesus instructed his disciples to do. If your classmates wouldn't listen to you when you warned them that what they are doing is not nice, just pick yourself up and dust yourself off." I hugged Grandmother, and she kissed me on both cheeks and on the forehead. Now I knew what to do.

At Academy Grade School, our fourth-grade class had been ice skating on the sidewalk, having a grand time. We applied layer after layer of water, forming a virtual ice rink in front of our school. Then we mastered the skills of graceful slides, including fancy turns to the left and to the right. However, one classmate definitely could not "slippyslidey" with the rest. Bob wore leg braces due to poliomyelitis. He could not run and was completely awkward when he tried to slide. We had all laughed at him, myself included. That was my dilemma. I knew it hurt Bob, and I did not want to do that. Dad, as a doctor, talked at suppertime of compassion and caring. Mom taught me not to tease my sisters. I was a slow learner, but she got the lesson through my thick skull.

Grandmother applied the icing on the cake. I knew that I could stand up for Bob even if others taunted me. So the next day, I stood by Bob. His friendship meant more than a greased lightning slide down the walk. He accepted my apology for laughing at him. To this day we remain friends, often working together at Camp Tommy, a camp for children of all ages who have special needs. I'm so glad my grandmother taught me to show tender, loving care.

WHIPPOORWILL CALLS

"Pucker up." Mom demonstrated with a big kiss on my cheek. I did want to whistle like Mom and Dad, and especially wanted to whistle the song of the whippoorwill. But I did not want to learn how to kiss. At five years of age, I did not want to be a sissy.

"Shape your aperture like this," Dad demonstrated, using a doctor's term which pleased me. Someday I'd grow up and be just like Dad, I told myself and God when I said my bedside prayers before climbing in and pulling the blankets over my body.

"Now blow out," both Mom and Dad commanded.

Gleefully I made a whistling sound. Now we grew silent as we sat on the picnic table in the near dark. We listened until we heard the call of the whippoorwill. How thrilling! This was how Mom would call us in when we played hide-and-go-seek until dusk. When she whistled, we ran home. The whippoorwill call was also how she signaled to Dad when he worked in the garden, letting him know it was time to come in and clean up for supper. In turn, Dad would whistle the whippoorwill call as he exited his car and walked toward the house, returning from a house call or from the hospital. How we all listened for the call of the whippoorwill!

Whip-poor-will
Whip-poor-will
Whip-poor-will

Many moons pass in life, but some rituals are unchanging. Summer nights and the call of the whippoorwill beckon us outside to see the starry heavens. Mom begins by pointing out constellations. "There is Orion, the Hunter. See the two hunting dogs, Ursa Major and Ursa Minor. For thousands of years, moms and dads have taught their children to look up to the heavens. See the Milky Way, the road of the gods." Mom would wave her arms across the sky.

"Now that is one big pancake!" I joke.

More moons pass.

"Dad, thanks for taking Butch, Gail, Bill, and me on our Boy Scout First Class overnight camp out," I say as I gesture, offering him burnt marshmallows on a cut stick, just cooked by our campfire. We have traveled to the remote Hemlock community where Dad took me on a house call following the death of my friend, Ricky Summers.

"Listen," Dad says. "Hear the call of the whippoorwill!"

More moons pass.

K, Anne, Ruthie, Bethie, Mom, Dad, and I gather for our Fourth of July campout at the Wilderness, our farm getaway in Hemlock. The restored log cabin is a safe place to sleep, but first we linger around the campfire, listening to the call of the whippoorwill and looking for constellations. I can always find Orion with his belt, but my imagination stops there.

K reflects, "The Prince Charming whom I marry must want to come camping at the Wilderness." Then dreamy-eyed, K recalls the thick emerald moss at the deep edge of the forest and exclaims, "And he must want to make love on the moss!"

More moons pass.

West Virginia University Behavioral Medicine and Psychiatry residency staff and fellow residents accept my invitation to visit my roots for a camping experience at our family's now very dear Wilderness farm. Paul Hlusko, MD, child psychiatrist, challenged me on grand rounds to never cross the state line of West Virginia. He opined that I could have a record for being the most educated West Virginian who never left home. He knew of my roots in the heart of

West Virginia, my undergraduate education at West Virginia Wesleyan College, my medical school education at West Virginia University, and now my postgraduate residency in Psychiatry in Charleston, West Virginia. This time, my girlfriend Araceli is also along for the adventure. She has brought her guitar to sing "Take Me Home, Country Roads," a song her mother in the Philippine Islands sings with John Denver on the radio. Once again, we gather in the twilight around the embers of our campfire and listen to the call of the whippoorwill.

More moons pass.

Dad pronounces that he has enjoyed the practice of medicine; that he has been blessed with a wonderful wife who now has passed on to the other side three years earlier; that he has written his memoirs; and that he is ready to eat strawberries from his patch as a final meal. Indeed, he dies as if by decree in the middle of the afternoon, in his own bed, surrounded by K, a pastor; Thom, a chaplain; Beth, a nurse; Araceli, a doctor; and me, a doctor. We are holding hands and are in prayer. His faithful dog is vigilant at the bedside.

Late into the evening I find myself sitting on the porch swing, enveloped in comfortable darkness below a giant hemlock tree. What I experience cannot be explained but is very real.

"Greenbrier," my dad is calling my name.

I listen intently. My grief is acute; I want to hear Dad once again call my name.

I feel the wind blow around me.

I hear the wind rustle through the overhanging hemlock.

"Carry on," the wind blows.

Once more, the whippoorwill calls.

THE TEN COMMANDMENTS OF MOTHER

I: Thou shalt be kind.

II: Thou shalt clean up your own mess.

III: Thou shalt help in the garden.

IV: Thou shalt develop your talents.

V: Thou shalt not smoke nor drink.

VI: Thou shalt do chores first, then play.

VII: Thou shalt stop, visit, honk, and help with chores at the grandparents' house.

VIII: Thou shalt write thank-you notes.

IX: Thou shalt clean your plate. (If peas are passed to Greenbrier first, pass his plate on around the table because he hogs the peas.)

X: Thou shalt be allowed to stay up a bit later as you grow up. (Half an hour extra as a 10-year-old meant reading the *World Book Encyclopedia* from A to Z, half an hour at a time.)

THE TEN COMMANDMENTS OF FATHER

I: Thou shalt listen to a good story, especially at bedtime.

II: Thou shalt be home for suppertime, family-style.

III: Thou shalt learn all 212 human bones, with some actual skeleton parts used as props, by the age of five.

IV: Thou shalt take swimming lessons at West Pool every summer until you swim well enough to pass the Boy Scout's First Class requirement.

V: Thou shalt mow a lot of grass every summer—play comes after the chores.

VI: Thou shalt study hard, "family-style." Everyone reads his or her book for a spell then shares what has been learned.

VII: Thou shalt listen to gory details of operations, close calls in deliveries, ER traumas, and snake bites at the supper table.

VIII: Thou shalt obey Mom, for she is Boss.

IX: Thou shalt not tease your sisters, and thou shalt protect them on walks through City Park.

X: Thou shalt accompany Dad on house calls and carry the doctor's bag.

Cardinalis cardinalis

WEST VIRGINIA
State Bird

FRIENDS

THE KING AND THE PRESIDENT

Elvis Presley is King. Rock 'n' roll is young, and so are Steve and I. We are best of friends from the get-go. His mom has invited me over to their Smithfield Street home after school, and my mom has said yes. The gingerbread snaps and cold milk hit the spot. Learning reading, writing, and arithmetic is hard work. We finish our snack as Mrs. Brown returns to her soap operas and her ironing.

Steve wants to show me his room, so up the steps we bound. He has just purchased a new 45 rpm record from Murphy's Five and Dime. His dad, our local B&O train engineer, has given Steve a record player. This makes Steve the most popular kid in Mrs. Olive Baxa's second-grade class. Steve declares that someday he will run for class president, and I can run his campaign. To celebrate the moment, we spin the King singing his hit "Hound Dog." We have watched black and white television with Elvis swinging his hips and gyrating wildly. So we jump up on Steve's bed and begin bopping and bouncing to the beat. Higher and higher! Wilder and wilder! We are dancing. Life is good. A friendship of a lifetime is born.

And yes, Steve became president of the Buckhannon-Upshur High School Class of 1966.

RICKY

The summer between the fourth and fifth grade, Elma and Cliff Summers lost their son in a farming accident out on Brushy Fork Road. I lost my best friend.

Ricky and I had shared secrets like little boys love to do. We had cut our wrists and touched our bleeding wounds together—we were blood brothers. We both had the same fourth-grade teacher, Miss Cookman. She loved me, and I read all 174 of her library books. I could do the schoolwork quickly, so I sat near the bookcase in the back of the room and read while other kids finished their work. Ricky, on the other hand, sat up by Miss Cookman's desk. He was always in trouble. He squirmed too much. He did not read well. He did not do math well. There was a possibility he was going to have to repeat the fourth grade.

But during recess, Ricky played the best of any other boy in my class. He had a tremendous imagination. We could really get into Cowboys and Indians. Or we could travel to Mars, as Miss Pickle did in one of Miss Cookman's books. But Ricky's favorite game was to act out what we learned in Sunday school. He would take the place of Jesus and hang on the Cross. Or, as Mother more properly noted, Jesus took Ricky's place on the Cross and died so Ricky could go to heaven.

Ricky longed for heaven. His farm was a sort of heaven for him. He wanted to share it with me as soon as "the teachers let the mules out," as we loved to sing about the end of school. Ricky and I constantly talked of camping on his farm. He had told me that Jesus talked to him; he knew he was going to heaven someday. So when I learned that Ricky had died on his family farm, I also knew in my heart that he was in heaven. My mother explained how I could be in heaven someday, as she explained that Ricky was. Accepting Jesus into my heart was a decision that changed my life.

MY BEST FRIEND DANNY

Danny and I played together every day. Sometimes I ran up the hill to play Cowboys and Indians around the Daniel's home and barn. One time I was making a getaway after robbing a pretend bank. Danny was in hot pursuit. I jumped their hemlock hedge and landed hard on my chest, which knocked the breath out of me. Danny was prepared to perform CPR to revive me. He was that kind of friend.

Sometimes Danny ran down the hill to play in our sandbox. One time we had a big road construction project going. We were building a tunnel through a mountain; Danny was on one side and I was on the other. When we did not meet in the middle as planned, we started throwing sand at each other. Finally, we were crying in frustration. Danny ran home, vowing never to come back. After lunch we were best friends again.

We shared secrets of life. One time we found a box turtle and decided we would boil it, making turtle soup. Our hearts were set on it until Mrs. Lena Stansberry told us the turtle heart would keep on beating outside the body. In fact, if we ate the heart, it would beat inside of us, she declared. She was a lifesaver to that turtle.

Danny had traits that I admired. Whatever he could imagine, he could build. One time we decided to be like Huckleberry Finn and Jim, floating down the Buckhannon River to the Tygart River, to the Monongahela River, to the Ohio River, and clear down the Mississippi River. Danny and I made a raft/rowboat. His dad, a master carpenter, made sure it was waterproof. How proud Danny and I were when we christened our boat "Friends Forever," launching it near Pringle Tree Park and floating clear to the Hall Bridge.

Danny played in the Buckhannon-Upshur High School Band. He played an excellent baritone while I played trombone. Never have brass horns blended as well as ours did. Danny even made All-State Band.

At West Virginia Wesleyan College, Danny and I double-dated the night he met Becky. I was there when my best friend fell in love. Later I was honored to be his best man. He even forgave me for bringing us out of the side door of St. Mary's United Methodist Church a hymn too early to meet his bride. Reverend McCune, his father-in-law, graciously handed us a hymn book to join in the singing rather than twiddle our thumbs.

How happy I have been to call Danny my best friend. When West Virginia Governor Gaston Caperton recognized Danny as an outstanding teacher and innovator in teaching with computer technology, and West Virginia Wesleyan College recognized him with their Alumni Award, I clapped the loudest.

The following year, seeing Danny pictured on the cover of the Chesapeake and Potomac Telephone Book, featuring teaching with technology, gave me a mountaintop high, knowing we had played together every day and shared a childhood of sweet memories.

Having a best friend like Danny—who could ask for anything more?

DARING TO DO THE DIFFICULT

Danny and I did not mind crooked trails that led to amazing views. We climbed Mount Hibbs, which overlooks Buckhannon, summer, fall, winter, and spring. Sledding down at a breakneck speed was par for the course many a stormy winter day when school was canceled. Most of the time we were not hurt during our semi-dangerous escapades. Best friends through thick and thin, Danny and I shared a challenge.

One spring day when I was in the fifth grade, we decided to set up an Olympic Track and Field course in the Daniel's cow pasture. We had played baseball there in the past and knew we could avoid cow paddies and other obstacles. Indeed, we had a grand course which included a 100-yard dash, as well as a javelin throw that was particularly thrilling since we threw downhill and over a ravine with Olympic Gold range.

We did our homework well, learning how to construct hurdles that would give way if accidentally knocked down. We knew the college hurdle at 42 inches was too high, as would be the high school standard of 39 inches. We wanted nothing to do with the women's high hurdle which was 33 inches. So we set our standard hurdle at 30 inches, and the low hurdle and youth hurdle at 27 inches.

Making a house call with Dad to an older couple, the lady had asked me about my interests. She was hard of hearing. When I said that my best friend and I were setting up an Olympic Track and Field course for the kids of Buckhannon, she got excited. But she couldn't understand why we wanted to jump "turtles"! Oh how Danny and I laughed when I told him later. It just inspired me to be a champion hurdle jumper.

Finally we were ready to test our track. The day was rainy and the clouds were so low that the fog was palpable. That should have been a warning that the grass could be wet and thus slippery. Danger never crossed our minds. Our heads were in the clouds, literally and figuratively. When my turn came to test our 100-yard dash with the youth height hurdles, I ran like the honor of the United States of America was on the line. Bringing home the Gold was my goal. No obstacle could stop me. Raw speed was my forte.

No stutter steps for me. I followed the three-step technique. Boy, was I flying! On the third hurdle, I slipped on a fresh cow paddy. It upended me, sending both feet ahead over the hurdle. My arms were swinging wildly like a bird attempting to fly. The landing was hard. Still basically left-handed, I attempted to catch myself. Again a snap. Again a fractured radius. I had broken my left arm a second time.

The arm healed well, but my interest turned from track and field to trombone playing, which I began with a right-handed slide. Danny agreed to play the baritone. We took another crooked trail together, daring to do the difficult by making music.

E PLURIBUS UNUM

"Out of many, one." Our national motto, "E Pluribus Unum," will be an important lesson for me to teach our grandchildren. How did I learn this lesson of unity and teamwork?

From church kindergarten on, I have been aware that I had a mirror image person in my life. What is that kind of person? The concept began to take shape for me in the Sunday comics. Mom used to read them to me. She'd say, "Now it is time for your education!" Mandrake the Magician was a favorite. He would stand in front of a mirror, looking at his handsome figure in a tux with a red cape. Just like me, I imagined. Then he'd perform magic. He'd put his hand on the glass and press gently. His hand, then his arm, and finally his whole body, would slip into the mirror and into another world on the other side. It was pure magic, and I loved the concept.

A little girl named Cay, who was in Sunday school with me, became my own mirror image person.

* First, Cay was a girl and I was a boy.
* Second, Cay had only brothers and I had only sisters.
* Third, Cay lived on one side of Water Tank Hill and I lived on the other side.
* Fourth, Cay loved to play Cowboys and Indians, taking the part as a cowgirl. I loved to play, but I preferred to be an Indian.
* Finally, Cay had a loud mouth and was outgoing; on the other hand, I was quiet and even shy.

We grew up knowing each other like the palms of our hands. We knew the same nursery rhymes. One we sang, but which I did not really understand, went like this: "Fire on the mountain; run boys run!"

Our day of "E Pluribus Unum" came the day

Water Tank Hill caught on fire. From all the steeping in Mother Goose, both of us instinctively knew what to do when the white billows of smoke rose over our dividing mountain.

We ran up the steep slope toward the fire to help put it out. Cay ran from her side. I ran from mine. We grabbed wet rags and followed the lead of firemen, slapping at the burning grass and shrubs. For what seemed like hours, we worked together, beating the fire and smoke.

We laughed.
We sweated.
We grew grungy with ash together.
When the fire was finally extinguished, we had bonded.
E Pluribus Unum.

Cay and I shared the memory at our 45th B-UHS Reunion in May 2011, both marveling at what happened to us that day.

LIKE KISSING YOUR SISTER

Boy, was I excited!!! Dad came home from St. Joseph's Hospital in his green Willys Jeep and announced that he had a surprise for us. We had just gathered around the kitchen table for supper. Mom stood by Dad and seemed to be in the know. What was the secret? K, Anne, Ruthie, and I yelled out in unison, "Show us! Show us! Show us!"

Dad left our small kitchen and returned in a moment, standing next to something covered carefully in a blanket. Dramatically, he pulled back the top and announced, "We have a new sister!" Oh my! This was not my idea of a surprise; I already had three sisters. Her name was Dwanda. She gave us a shy look. What was she thinking?

Mom told us we would need to share and share alike. We soon were laughing and telling Mom and Dad and Dwanda about our adventures around our neighborhood. Today we explored more of the Enchanted Forest, a large crab apple thicket where surely Sleeping Beauty lived in a hidden castle. We climbed Mount Hibbs, the highest point in Buckhannon. Our next project would be to build a tree house in the highest tree. We rode our horse Pinto Scout, all of us at the same time, up Leonard Holler to a flowing stream where we built dams. Dwanda would have to join us tomorrow on our many adventures. As it turned out, she was quite a cowgirl when we played Cowboys and Indians. And she was really adept at hide-and-go-seek. Best of all, she could really hit a long ball and run fast when we played baseball with the rest of the hilltop gang.

Having Dwanda as a sister was not half bad. A week of summer fun went by quickly. So what a surprise when Mom and Dad announced at supper that Dwanda had a real home. The next day she would be leaving us. She was surprised herself. Girls are hard to figure out. She laughed and cried at the same time. As it turned out, her mom, a nurse, had given birth to a baby. Her dad was busy caring for their other children and for his insurance business, so all the hospital staff had decided to be good neighbors. "The love of Christ urges us on" was the hospital motto. This was taken to heart by the nurses and doctors. For the Almond family, Dwanda may have been the first but was not the last to come and stay a spell. Mom and Dad stopped counting at 99. Above our door a signed was posted: "You enter a stranger only once!"

Years later when Dwanda and I were entering our teenage years, I asked her out to the movies. *Tammy*, starring Debbie Reynolds, was the summer flick. I met her mom and dad in their living room. I reassured them we would walk straight home from the Kanawha Theater three blocks down Kanawha Street from their family home/insurance office. Certainly I was proud to pay 20 cents for each ticket and to buy popcorn for a dime. I earned the money weeding the garden and mowing grass. We had a good time, but I never asked Dwanda out again. It was too much like kissing your sister.

Acer saccharum
WEST VIRGINIA
State Tree

© Noel W. Tenney 95

COMMUNITY LIFE

WE ARE THE CHURCH

Togetherness is how I remember our family. Getting ready for church on Sunday began on Saturday evening with Dad polishing shoes and Mom laying out the clothes we would wear. She was an excellent seamstress, so these were homemade clothes that she cut from the same cloth.

Sunday proved to be special in other ways, too. After the church service, Clark's Grocery would open briefly so that families like ours could stop by to purchase our dessert—a quart of Imperial ice cream. We enjoyed a chicken dinner prepared by our neighbor, Lena Stansberry, giving Mom a day off from cooking. Often we invited the pastor and his family, or perhaps a West Virginia Wesleyan College professor and his family, to join us.

The afternoons proved refreshing on Sundays. We could expect an excursion to swim in the Buckhannon River, or to hike as a family up through the neighborhood to the top of Mount Hibbs. Everyone had a grand time on Sunday, especially Brier, our collie dog, who knew that the table scraps tasted better. Dad would teach Brier to talk by barking for his treats. We laughed more on Sundays, and we grew together, loving God and our neighbor.

Following are some snapshots of my growing up in Buckhannon's First United Methodist Church.

ONE

Memory is mostly tied to our sense of smell. I recall Mrs. Icey Smallridge, my kindergarten teacher, down in the basement classroom where the choir dresses today. She had the strongest lilac perfume ever. We had many great times, including playing games on the expansive Shannon lawn (now Frank Hartman's home). I looked forward to Sunday School except for one thing: from May 1st on, we could run barefoot all summer long up on the hill behind the City Park. On Sundays, however, we had to wear shoes. My, my, how they confined my feet!

TWO

Bill Hornbeck and I were good friends. When the church decided to start using the youth as acolytes, we were selected to be the first. His grandmother, Pauline Dutton, whose Elm Street home was where Ron and Peg McCauley live now, dressed us up in white robes and tied big black bows around our necks each week. This was 55 years ago, but it seems like yesterday. The hard part, besides dressing up, was sitting in the front row. Reverend Samuel Harford preached very well-organized sermons; at Sunday dinner my parents would dissect them. Dad said he spent 40 hours each week getting the sermon just right. They were a bit above my head. Actually, just over my head from the front row perspective!!!

THREE

Boys and girls had separate Sunday School classes. We had opening exercises with lots of singing. "This is My Father's World" was one of our favorites. In seventh grade, my Buckhannon-Upshur Junior High principal, Lemar Bond, was also my Sunday School teacher. He was very wise. One time a classmate said he wanted to be a truck driver. Lemar Bond agreed that this was honest work, but he strongly suggested to us all that we should plan on going to college. Once we were well educated, we could still become truck drivers if we chose, but could also fall back on our education. However, it would be difficult to do it vice versa. A person who aspired to be a truck driver would have difficulty moving on to being a teacher, a lawyer, a doctor, or other professional. I never forgot the lesson!!!

FOUR

First United Methodist Church has some of the most ornate and colorful stained glass windows imaginable. I recently led the boys of Cub Scout Pack 128 on a tour of the church for our yearly "God and Me" and "God and Family" projects. I need not have been surprised when one little Scout exclaimed, "These Christians love us!"

"How is that?" I asked quizzically.

"See the Scout sign in all the windows!" the perceptive Cub pointed out.

Indeed, the fleur-de-lis, which is the Scout emblem, appears again and again in the stained glass design. In addition to being used as the sign of a Scout, this emblem is also at the end of a mariner's compass. And of course, Jesus Christ is often named the Lily of the Valley. How wonderfully Scouting, the love of Christ, and a passion for excellence have come together in our church family.

In my own childhood, Pat Nickell and Betty Weimer carried the Scouting banner well.

FIVE

My first Scoutmaster, Pat Nickell, led us boys of Troop 128, which is one of the oldest troops in West Virginia. We held our meetings at the church. The troop has produced many Eagle Scouts, including myself. The beginning, however, can be delicate.

My mother would read nursery rhymes to us five children. I was the lone boy among four sisters. One poem attempted to explain the difference between boys and girls:

"What are little girls like? Sugar and spice and everything nice. What are little boys like? Snakes and snails and puppy dog tails."

I would actually cry as my sisters teased me. I felt the description of boys was too crude. But when you get to hike and camp with boys, the play can get pretty rough. I remember that my friend Bill Hornbeck was a heavy sleeper. In the middle of the night on a camping trip, we quietly picked up his army cot, with Bill in the cot sound asleep. We carried it to the stream and put him in the middle of the water. We knew he would be upset when he awoke and stepped out of bed, getting wet. We thought it was a great prank. Bill took it well, but some boys probably would have quit Scouts over such shenanigans.

Scoutmaster Pat was one of the tallest men I had ever known. He had a quick smile and a loud commanding voice. We would line up for inspection and recite the Scout Law and Promises, as well as the Pledge to the American Flag. Learning to tie the square knot and to cook peach cobbler to perfection sold me on Scouting in the fifth grade. Pat was such a great encourager, and joining Scouts was one of the decisions that changed my life.

SIX

Betty Weimer led the Girl Scouts. Each summer they had
day camp in Buckhannon City Park. Our family lived just
beyond the park. Always curious, I wanted to see what the
girls were up to, so I snuck through the woods to their
campsite. Boys were verboten, and I was spotted by some
girls, who yelled out an alarm. But Cay Canfield, the
daughter of Valta Canfield, who just celebrated her 90th
birthday with us, also saw me coming. She yelled out,
"That's not a boy, that's just Greenie!!!" To this day,
whenever Betty Weimer, who also just celebrated her 90th
birthday, sees me, she yells out, "That's just Greenie!!!"

SEVEN

Methodist Youth Fellowship expanded my ideas and beliefs. We had our District Camp at Selbyville, with 140 churches represented. We had the State MYF conferences at Jackson's Mill and West Virginia Wesleyan College. I loved every minute of it. Jim Knorr and his ventriloquist's figure, Iggy, would come to entertain and inspire us. Arnold Nelson, a psychology professor at WVWC, and his wife Rosemary supervised us. Incidentally, they also wrote *Haven in the Hardwood*, a book which recounts the history of Pickens, West Virginia.

We also had associate pastors, including Ron and Peg McCauley, who enhanced our vision. One time we gathered to learn "Your God is Too Small," our theme for the weekend conference at the First Methodist Church of Clarksburg. I was challenged by the speaker and the topic. Thanks to the youth ministry, my God WAS getting bigger!!!

CLOSE COUNTS

Growing up on the hill overlooking Buckhannon had many advantages, not the least of which was the neighborhood closeness. Evenings after supper we would gather as a community at the horseshoe pit. The men would pitch and the women would chat. All of the kids would play tag, hide-and-go-seek, and Red Rover.

Clang

The horseshoe pitched struck the stake. The rhythm of the game then called for a bit of conversation, as the moment of the pitch had required strict silence and great concentration.

"Senator Kennedy is running for President."

Clang

"He promises that all the roads will be straightened in West Virginia."

Clang

"And all the roads will be downhill!"

Clang

Four pitches and points counted. Ringer—three points. Leaner—one point. Six inches or closer—one point. Even as I played with the hilltop gang of kids, we listened to our dads and moms talk about the major issues of our day. They would solve the world's problems. Sometimes they threw dead ringers.

Rose and Raymond were childless. With the baby boom

following World War II, this seemed like a tragedy to the neighbors.

Clang

"We are adopting a little boy and a little girl."

Clang

"Some children are orphaned with no one to love them."

Clang

"We can all love the kids, together."

Clang

"We can build extra rooms on the house, together."

Clang

Close counts in horseshoes. Score a point.
Close counts in neighborliness. Score a point.

Clang

FRED AND GUS

The rituals and rhythms of small town life give comfort. Spring plowing and garden preparing fondly remind me of my parents and grandparents, who took infinite pains to get the tomato seeds growing in the windowsill box; who poured over the *Burpee Seed Catalogue* in anxious anticipation on the coldest winter day; who consulted the Farmer's Almanac to decide on the best day for plowing; and who alerted Fred and Gus that their services would definitely be needed.

"A time to plant, and a time to pluck up that which is planted" (Ecclesiastes 3:2) is just as spiritual to me as John 3:16, the "good news" verse:

"For God so loved the world, that he gave his only begotten Son, that whosoever believeth in him should not perish, but have everlasting life."

Each morning required a check with the thermometer hanging just outside the kitchen window. Is the temperature coming up? The *Buckhannon-Record* radio broadcast of the local news at 8:45 brought welcome news from Dr. Arthur Gould, the West Virginia Wesleyan College chemistry professor, who reported daily precipitation of rain or snow. At breakfast, Dad would turn to Mom and say, "When the chance of frost is past, I'm ready to pull the straw off the strawberries so the blossoms can get sunlight."

"Just wait a bit, Honey!" Mom would caution.

Spring had really sprung when Fred and Gus arrived to plow our six gardens, basically on any flat portions of our ten acres of hilltop heaven on earth. Dad, with a twinkle in his eye, would quiz us. "Who is Fred and who is Gus?" Which was the horse and which was the man? We always spoke of the two as if inseparable. I never really knew which was which.

Fred and Gus had already been plowing. Most folks in Buckhannon had a garden, and we all needed help turning over the rich soil of our delta. Eons of time, repeated flooding of the valley by the meandering river, and plenty of manure gave us rich gardens with a sweet smell that signaled all is right with the world.

My role as deep hole digger for the tomatoes pleased me. I built muscles and increased my strength at the same time as growing giant tomatoes. The hole had to be 3 feet deep. The aged cow manure brought from a farmer/patient filled the first foot of the hole. Sandy loam came next, followed by the homegrown tomato plant grown from seeds of the largest tomatoes of the past season. Around the plant, dirt gathered from under walnut trees in the woods finished the masterpiece.

The proof came in the harvest. Big, juicy tomatoes pressed between Grandmother Flanagan's homemade bread. Spaghetti sauce turned into Mom's famous porcupine meatballs. Tomato soup chunky style, with yellow, red, and orange tomatoes blended into a spicy concoction.

The garden always began with the help of Fred and Gus.

MINISTER WITHOUT PORTFOLIO

"Charlie, what do you do anyway?" I asked Charlie Beer as we gathered around our new brick backyard grill we were just completing. He certainly could use a cement trowel well. He buttered the two long sides and two short sides of the red bricks in two smooth motions and popped brick upon brick until the grill took form, then struck the joints, working in the mortar with the skill of a surgeon.

"Well, little Doc, I like to eat." Mom had noticed and commented to me that Dad's friend Charlie and his family would often show up for a visit and would normally be asked to stay for supper, as was common in those days. Mom did not mind, as we always prepared for an extra person or two. His wife Hazel, his daughter Jane, who was a year younger than I, and his son "little Tom" would make themselves at home. They laughed a lot. Charlie laughed loudest.

Charlie would often accompany Dad on all-night house calls to Helvetia, Alexander, Spruce Falls, Alton, Ten Mile, Tallmansville, Pickens, and other fairly remote locations. He could fix about any piece of mechanical equipment, whether it be a garden rototiller, a lawn mower, or Doc's green Jeep that climbed the roads, creeks, and paths to patients' homes that saw infrequent visits of wheeled vehicles. A flat tire, a bent wheel, a broken wire, or a broken axle could be deadly serious in a snowstorm. Mom felt better knowing "fix-it Charlie" was along.

"You know, little Doc, you can eat more standing up! The hamburger and fries drop clear to your feet. Then you can have seconds and thirds," Charlie laughed. "Haaaaa...Ha-Ha-Ha." Charlie always laughed the long-short- short- short belly laugh of a man who was really finding himself utterly witty and terribly amusing, whether the rest of the audience appreciated the humor or not.

"Seriously though, I'm Doc's sidekick. I ride shotgun in

his Jeep. I'm his sounding board. When he has his brilliant ideas, he tells me first. In government, the most important person besides the President of the United States is his minister without portfolio."

"Oh yeah. Nora Amundsen, my sixth-grade French teacher, taught us about 'Ministre Sans Portefeuille,'" I expounded. "Just like Danny Daniel is my best friend and secret keeper up on the Hill."

Over the years, Charlie was always there for our family. Dad asked him to teach me how to drive when I turned 16 years old. Dealing with automobile accidents and car repairs all across the state in his job as an insurance adjuster, Charlie was well acquainted with the dangers and results of automotive ineptitude and bad choices. His favorite little ditty was, "Don't be caught sitting dead on your seat belt," and he quipped it every time he entered an automobile. Many lessons that he taught have stood the test of time. I learned to drive on a three-speed standard transmission using a clutch, which made driving an automatic transmission a piece of cake. And just letting me stop and start on West Virginia hills, or navigating the rolling curves on Sago Road near Hampton, has been worth all the gold in Fort Knox. Allowing coal trucks and faster vehicles to pass me as I maintain focus on my lane and what is happening in front and behind me has saved my life several times. He taught me parallel parking, and also instructed me on changing tires and checking fluid levels. "If you take care of it now, you won't have to fix it later" was another one of Charlie's axioms.

Buckhannon-Upshur football became a phenomenon in the 1960s, with West Virginia State Championships in 1963, 1966, and 1969. Victoria Hill kitchen conferences with Football Coach Granville Zopp; Charlie, minister without portfolio; Dad, B-UHS Football team physician, and me listening in, quiet as a church mouse, are treasured memories. The trio—Coach, Sidekick, and Doc—analyzing football plays at our kitchen table taught me how men strategize. Our fireplace had a warm wood fire blazing, and the war room plots were hatched. The strengths of individual players, noted. The opposing side's weakest links, noted. Teaching ran even into the way that men deal with lopsided football victories like the 90 to 0 battle of Buckhannon-Upshur versus Shinnston game in 1963. That game taught several lessons on life, including the importance of humility and fair play from the perspective of looking in the rearview mirror.

My role in the football seasons was as yearbook photographer. Lynn Westfall, the very precise and learned English teacher who supervised the yearbook staff, wanted one good picture from each twelve-picture film roll. Budgets were tight, and processing cost money. Mr. Westfall wanted effectiveness from his photographer. By hearing play strategy around the dining table, I learned to anticipate Coach Zopp's play-by-play calls, thus capturing some really terrific sports photos.

The final chapter for Charlie and Dad is sad, as are all final chapters, but somehow appropriate. How poignant, Charlie's passing. He had driven an hour south of town to the recently completed Corps of Engineers Sutton Lake and Reservoir. On his return near the French Creek Game Farm, he must have sensed some dread and pain. Men commonly speak of feeling "the big one." Charlie, always the conscientious driver, pulled safely over to the side of the road in his metallic blue 1967 Ford Galaxy with his boat in tow. He died right there still in the driver's seat, his enlarged athletic heart having given out. By chance, the next vehicle coming down the road was Doc in his little green Jeep. He was returning from a call to vaccinate the residents of the remote communities of Helvetia and Pickens, his daughters Beth and Ruthie serving as his able assistants, although Beth was only 9 years old and Ruthie about 13. Dad stopped, recognizing Charlie's vehicle, and walked to the car window and said, "What's up Charlie?" Then with as much pain as if a brother had departed, Dad realized that his friend was gone. Dad went back to his Jeep, wondering how to compose himself and tell Charlie's family that their indestructible father had died. Overcome with grief, Dad stayed a spell with Charlie, knowing there was nothing that could be done for his friend. The next vehicle to stop on the scene was West Virginia State Trooper "Judd" Phillips, Charlie's good friend and neighbor on Brushy Fork. Next along Route 20 came Willard "Soupy" Campbell, another of the close friends that had been made by living and working and conferring for years in the same small town in those valleys formed by tall mountains and fast rivers. Together, they all held one last conference with Charlie; to the end he stayed his course, serving as minister without portfolio.

A special thanks to Tom Beer ("little Tom" in the story) for his collaboration with me on this story.

HOME HARDWARE
"Where Home and Hardware Needs Are Met"

Doc loved projects. All the hilltop kids of West Victoria Street loved the goldfish pond project, too. The idea on this day would be that we'd dig out the wet weather spring over the hill in a small cove. We'd dig down about 5 feet and make the circumference about 4 feet. What fun—getting gooey and muddy, staying cool in the summer sun. Then we'd pile into Doc's Jeep and go downtown for a Dairy Queen soft serve ice cream cone, followed by a shopping trip to Home Hardware. With the oily hardwood floors, this was one place where "no shoes, no shirt, no service" did not apply. We could come as we were.

Our project could be completely supplied by Herb Stalnaker and the rest of the Home Hardware crew. We needed an old wooden barrel which we would position down in our hole after we put rocks in the bottom for drainage. Around the outside of the barrel we would put the rebar that we also could buy at Home Hardware. Yes, they had cement with sand and gravel mixed in, and they also had it without. Whatever you want, just ask at Home Hardware. "If we don't have it, you don't need it!" a sign read near the potbelly stove strategically positioned in the middle of the store. Already on another hot day we had driven to the Buckhannon River near Ten Mile, where we gathered rock and sand, and also swam in a deep blue hole that local boys said had no bottom. Someday we were coming back to find the bottom, Dad said. What fun we had with our project.

By the time my youngest sister Bethie, our farmer neighbor's youngest child Donna, and I, along with Doc, arrived at Home Hardware, we were quite a sight. Painted like Indians with mud. Sticky faces and hands from melting ice cream. And really rambunctious.

True to their word, all supplies were found, and then

were loaded in the back of the Jeep. "Red," as folks called Dad because of his red hair, "we thank you for your business," said Herb Stalnaker as he made change, continuing to eye us. "Is there anything else I can help with you with?"

A big smile crossed by Dad's face as he contemplated his motley crew. He signaled for me to zipper my lips. Dad replied, "Why yes, Herb, you called me 'Red' and you are right. You also see that I have one little brunette child with me" (pointing to Bethie) "and one little redhead child" (pointing to Donna). "Which one is my daughter?"

Dad was always known for his quizzes, and so Herb, rubbing his head a bit, puzzled but did not back down. "Doc, I reckon I can't rightly say. Lois your wife is a brunette and you are a redhead." We all laughed and enjoyed the moment.

Later Donna told her mom about her adventures and about Doc's question. She told us her mother looked flabbergasted, then her face turned as red as her own red hair. "Listen, Honey, Doc is not your daddy!" she exclaimed.

"BEST CATCH YA EVER SEEN"
Being Paid by the Barter System

Fishing in the mountain streams yields brook trout, brown trout, and even stocked golden trout. On the first day of fishing season in the spring, one or more of Dad's patients would come to town with a string of fish. Mom preferred to have fish on Fridays, so this payment-in-full was heaven sent. Our kitty lived off table scraps, so this would be a cat's delight to her. Dad cautioned us not to feed Brier Dog fish because of the fine bones that could get caught in his throat.

One memorable day in 1960, patients from the Indian Camp community brought us a mess of fish, completing the doctor/patient barter transaction. Dad was one of the few doctors who would make house calls. In late winter, about the time of a spring thaw, I had ridden shotgun to Bean's Mill to see a patient with belly pain and fever. We turned the hubs, putting the Jeep in four-wheel drive at the top of the canyon rim, cautiously driving down the rutted road. Icicles 12 feet high and looking like pipe organs flowed down from the mountainside. The valley looked ominous on the left, dropping as a cliff with no guard rail. Water flowed down the ruts, periodically cascading as a waterfall 600 feet to the B&O Railroad tracks hugging the Buckhannon River. Dad worried a lot about getting back up the mountain. The river was running high at the bottom, nearly overflowing the Works Progress Administration Depression-era concrete bridge. Maybe we would need to catch the coal train out of Pickens headed downstream for Buckhannon to get home, Dad speculated. Back when there had been passenger service, most of the locals preferred using the train. For 25 cents they could travel in style down and back.

We stopped at the last remaining house in Bean's Mill, walking across slab logs serving as a path over the muddy yard from the gate to the porch. Free-range chickens clucked and a big old hound barely moved, letting us climb over him and into the house. Inside all was dark but was dry and warm. Dad let me hold a flashlight as he examined the lady-of-the-home's abdomen. He expressed concern about an inflamed appendix about to rupture. He let me feel the "hard as a board" right lower quadrant that he identified as McBurney's point. Dad told the family the story of Dr. "Buttonhole" Cox, a West Virginia Wesleyan College graduate, who had a surgical practice in Washington, DC. Because he had very small fingers, he could make a very tiny incision, leaving a scar the size of a buttonhole. Showgirls flocked to him for elective surgery in order to "keep their assets."

This day, Dr. Basil Page would do a good appendectomy, but we had to get our patient to town. Relatives further up the hill had a team of horses that could pull our Jeep up the rutted canyon road to transport our patient. A party line phone was available to call Conard St. Clair to bring the hearse, which also served as an ambulance, to meet us at Indian Camp. "Doc, when the river is down and Panther Fork is running clear, the children and I are going to get you the best catch ya ever seen in payment for your services," the husband promised. Dad and he shook hands on it. Sure enough, surgery cured the problem, and the fish began to bite. We soon enjoyed a Friday trout fish fry.

One day 50 years later, for my television show, I visited two talking crows in the kitchen of a family living on the canyon rim high over the now deserted Bean's Mill. The lady of the home took the family Bible off the coffee table and showed me a treasured note written by Mom thanking the family for the wonderful gift of native trout.

HIGH PLACES

I have friends in low places and in high places. Let me reflect with you on three friends in high places. I know they have a reward in heaven. After all, the Bible tells me so: "Greater love hath no man than this, that a man lay down his life for his friends." (John 15:13)

RALPH

"A rose by any other name would smell as sweet."
                                                    -Shakespeare

My middle name is "Ralph." I am named for an uncle whom I never met. Uncle Ralph was flying Army Air Corps missions in World War II in the South Pacific somewhere near New Guinea when his plane was shot down by the Japanese. He was lost at sea but has a marker at the "Punchbowl," as the National Memorial Cemetery of the Pacific in the crater above Pearl Harbor is known. Mom and Dad often emphasized the above Scripture from the Gospel of John. Ralph, too, had "great love." He left behind a wife and young son. He left grieving sisters, a father, a stepmother, and my father. Ralph had a genius for engineering and mechanics. Dad recalled that as teenagers, they wanted to build a hot rod. This was in the Great Depression. There was no money. Not one to be deterred, Ralph said, "Let's go to the junkyard and see what we can see." He spied a dirty motor over in the corner of the junkyard, partly buried in mud and weeds. They bought it for a dime, and Uncle Ralph brought it back to life. It is an honor to bear the name "Ralph."

The rest of my name has a story, too. How many names do you know like Greenbrier David Ralph Almond??? But that is a story for another day.

ATTABOY, FRED

Fred Michael Kerns was one of the best friends any boy could have growing up in the West Virginia hills. We shared everything—4-H, a love of running, Methodist Youth Fellowship and Sunday School, small town life in Buckhannon, even the angst of acne and feeling like we were ugly and awkward around girls. We both had professional dads. His father was a telecommunications engineer and ran the telephone company, and mine was a country doctor frequently making house calls. Our families were well respected; we understood that. We had dreams. Fred wanted to be a dentist. I wanted to follow in my father's tracks and be a family doctor. We graduated in 1966, well aware of the Vietnam War. There were 315 of us in our Buckhannon-Upshur High School class. Of these, 150 young men volunteered for military service; 150 young women promised true love and waited for their return. Fifteen of us went to college. Fred selected Fairmont State College; I selected West Virginia Wesleyan College.

After the first year, both of us were struggling with grades. College is tough!!! Fred decided to join the United States Marine Corps, and I went to summer school. Fred served well as a US Marine in Vietnam for 13 months. He volunteered to teach kids in an orphanage about Jesus and about various 4-H projects. There he made a decision to adopt an orphan. All went well, but paperwork can take longer than expected. If he returned home after his tour, the adoption would fall through. Fred volunteered to re-up. The second month into his second tour, Fred died in a rice paddy in Vietnam, also showing "great love."

"Attaboy, Fred!" I hear a chorus of angels from heaven proclaim!!!

TERRY

Terry made it back from the war in Southeast Asia, but suffered from Post-Traumatic Stress Disorder. I treated him at the VA Medical Center until his untimely death in a motorcycle crash. Though I have had the high privilege to treat thousands of veterans, Terry stands out, as he was my first.

We met soon after I arrived on station at the Clarksburg VAMC in the fall of 1988. Terry and I shared a love of Hemlock, West Virginia. The Almond family farm is there. We call it "The Wilderness." That is what Hemlock is all about—hemlock trees and the world's greatest hardwood forest. The amount of rain also makes it a "rain forest," according to what Terry taught me.

Over the hill from Hemlock, Terry managed 12,000 acres for WestVaCo. He had used his GI Bill to go to forestry school at West Virginia University upon his discharge from military service. Terry discovered a cove of 400 acres of virgin timber, which he called his "Sanctuary." His dilemma was whether or not should he tell the "big wigs" in New York City who ran the company about his "Sanctuary." If he told, they would cut the trees. If he did not tell, they would fire him when they found out. Terry asked me to make a "house call" to his forest, which I was glad to do. We hiked along a mountain stream with waterfalls, going higher and higher. The Bunner family had logged here with the help of teams of horses a hundred years ago. The skid marks where they would slide timber down the mountainside to the stream was evident. However, there was a crown with a cove they could not easily reach, so they left it. The sight takes your breath away!!! We sat on a giant log toppled by time. "What to do?" we cogitated. Finally, I suggested that this was too rare a find not to disclose to headquarters; however, I saw a way out:

*75% of our medicines are from plants.
*West Virginia University can do basic science research here in "Terry's Sanctuary."
*WestVaCo can get a tax credit plus earn the good will of West Virginians.
*Terry can save his life by keeping his Sanctuary while helping to save mankind's health.

That is exactly what happened with Terry taking another risk. His first risk was volunteering to serve his country. His second risk was volunteering to serve humanity by creating a medicine research forest.

"Greater love has no man than this; that a man lay down his life for his friends."

SCHOOL

SIX SHOOTER

Happiness is a six shooter when a boy is six years old. Mom hated guns; she made that very clear. Dad did hunt some with his sidekick, Charlie Beer, but he always respected "whatever your mother said." Another version of that would be, "Ask your mother," whenever I'd come to Dad, figuring my chance of getting to "yes" was better with him.

However, on the 23rd of January, 1954, they agreed on two things for my birthday:

* Now is the time for me to have a watch.
* Now is the time to settle the six shooter issue.

How surprised and pleased I was when I tore open my birthday gift wrapping and opened one of my greatest gifts. There in a hard box was a Gene Autry six shooter watch with a picture of America's favorite singing cowboy hero on the face and a second hand that was a gun firing 120 shots per minute. I was in ecstasy.

On the playground, packs of boys and girls would gather around me to see the watch tick and the six shooter fire away. As part of our opening exercises, our first-grade class would sing Gene Autry's "Rudolph, the Red-Nosed Reindeer," as well as "Happy Birthday" to me on my special day.

Every day I'd get up early, wash my face, brush my teeth, and put my six shooter on my left wrist. Mrs. Strader expressed some concern that I was left-handed. She conceded that I printed my ABCs pretty well, but she made a disappointing face when I'd do it with my left hand.

From watching Cowboy and Indian movies on Grandmother's television on Saturday mornings, I realized that shooting from the hip with guns blazing right and left would be even more daring. I could get the bad guys twice as fast. So I'd practice holding my pencil and writing with both hands. After all, shooting with both hands was the main point. Dad, being a doctor, told me that I was becoming "ambidextrous." He said he learned 10,000 new words in medical school. He always taught us new words. Dad had also taught me the names of all 212 bones in the human body.

Life is so surprising. What happened next changed my life. Jeff and Jeanie Brooks moved in next door. Morgan Brooks, their dad, was actually building their home. We took to climbing high up on their scaffolding. Then we took to climbing the hemlock tree up at Mrs. Stansberry's home. We were becoming regular monkeys. I could even swing with one arm from limb to limb like a monkey. One May day we decided to climb all the apple trees in the Clark family farm orchard, just over the hill from our homes. We challenged each other to climb higher and to swing further.

I dare you!
I double dare you!
I double, double dare you!

We became more and more daring and reckless. Then it happened, a day I will always remember. One minute I was swinging like a monkey, and the next minute I was free falling toward the ground. To protect myself and to cushion my fall, I reached out my left arm. When I hit the ground, I heard a snap. My arm was broken. To be precise, my left radius bone was broken. More tragically, my Gene Autry six shooter watch was broken. My dismay could not be contained. My little heart was broken. Time stood still. Dad put me in a plaster of Paris cast and my radius healed. Mrs. Strader helped me finish the first grade as a right-hander.

And my next watch was a Timex.

MAUDE STRADER
Right from the Start

Maude Strader taught first grade at the Academy Grade School, giving a lifetime of excellent service. She gave teaching total devotion, truly 110%.

By the time my class came along in 1954, she was seasoned. What a privilege to be her student. But I never told her how special she has been in my life until one fall day many years later. For 40 years I ran daily. Usually I ran 4 to 6 miles in an hour of blissful freedom from doctoring. Buckhannon is a small mountain town on the western slopes of the Alleghenies. My head would be in the clouds but my feet on the ground. I ran here and there all over town. I could be a kid again when I ran. I could dream again that I was flying.

One day I ran by Mrs. Strader's home, hardly realizing that she sat alone on her porch. But in a moment of recognition, suddenly I became overcome with gratitude. The Spirit moves me. I have a saying that I tell myself: "Not only do I believe in miracles, I depend on them!" This day, the Spirit moved me to bound over to Mrs. Strader, who was sitting on her porch. I probably had not spoken to her since leaving her class. In my mind's eye she remained a tall, thin, proper, middle-aged school mum. As I drew near, she seemed to age in an instant. She sat there looking extremely thin. She had a dowager's hump. Though it was warm, she had a quilt lap blanket. As I began to speak, she cupped her hand to her ear, indicating she did not hear well. Her vision dim, she took both hands and grasped my cheeks and drew me near so she could study my face.

I began by giving my name and class year. I told her she was the best first-grade teacher ever. Her witty sayings written on the blackboard inspire my practice of psychotherapy to this day. A patient complains of manic exuberance and I reply, "All sun makes Sahara!" A dozen times a day I am back in Mrs. Strader's class, reflecting on her wisdom. I reminded her of how gracious she had been to let Sandra Johns, Sharlotte Pugh, and me sit in the back of the class together. At least twice a day we would get the giggles so profusely that we would disrupt her teaching. Even as she would eye us sternly, we would hold our laughter for a moment, then burst out laughing until we cried. Yet Mrs. Strader saw a reason to ignore us. Because of laughter we loved school.

Yes, Mrs. Strader, I told her, your reading circles were fun. Jim and Judy and Tags the dog are still my imaginary friends. "C-H-A-I-R." When I spelled "chair" correctly and won the spelling contest in first grade, I knew that I could do anything. Even today, that accomplishment is a proud moment in my educational life, climbing a steep ladder. My 12 years of secondary education, graduating from Buckhannon-Upshur High School in 1966, began on a bottom rung in Mrs. Strader's class. Then there would be 11 years of postgraduate education studying medicine and psychiatric specialty training. How encouraged I was to win the spelling bee. Thank you, Maude Strader!!!

What happened next is precious beyond compare. Mrs. Strader reached up, putting her arms around my neck, and hugged me tightly and kissed me on my forehead. She laughed and cried. We embraced for 10 minutes or more.

How blessed we are for great teachers who help us right from the start.

MIMEOGRAPH—I LOVE THE SMELL

Falling in love with a teacher may not be that rare. I've done it a few times myself. But what happened in the second grade confuses me even now. Did I fall in love with Olive Baxa, or did I just fall in love with the odor of the printing ink from her mimeograph?

Certainly she was a young teacher among the crop we had at Academy Grade School. Elegant like a Strawberry Festival Queen. Kind like my mother. Her parents were a retired Methodist minister and helpmeet like my own grandparents. And I became her "teacher's pet." What was there not to love?

"Greenbrier, I need some help tomorrow after school to mimeograph our arithmetic homework for the next school quarter. Will you help me?"

Mom had always told me to seek her and Dad's permission, but I felt sure they would say yes. I ran all the way home. No stopping to climb the maple tree at the top of Chestnut Street today. No stopping to build dams in the ditch by City Park. No pausing to curry our horse, Pinto Scout. No wrestling our collie, Brier Boy.

"Mother, may I? Mother, may I? Mother, may I?"

"Yes, you may!"

Mrs. Baxa said her mimeograph printing press was set up on her sun porch at her home on Barbour Street, two blocks from our school. I even carried her books home. We sang "West Virginia Hills," and I skipped as we made our way to her house. Thomas Edison invented the mimeograph machine, Mrs. Baxa taught me. He invented the incandescent light bulb. He invented the movie projector. Maybe I would be an inventor someday, Mrs. Baxa suggested. I liked the idea. I told her that Ben Franklin discovered electricity by flying a kite in a thunderstorm. He put a metal key between himself and the kite to avoid being electrocuted. I was proud to tell her what I knew. But I did not tattle on our hilltop kids hiking to Leonard Holler and grabbing hold of an electric fence. Adults, even a fine teacher like Mrs. Baxa, would not approve, especially if she knew that the big kids plotted to hold hands, placing the little kids on the end. We had discovered that when the biggest boy grabbed the electric fence, the shocking power would travel through his body to the next guy and on to the next guy, all the way down to the little kid on the end who would be the only one shocked.

Preparing for our project of mimeographing, Mrs. Baxa filled her printing press with ink. Already I knew that all the second-grade kids loved the smell of the ink. We would grab our papers as they were passed from the front to the back of the rows and lift them to our noses and take a big whiff. My, my!

Soon the sunny room was filled with the fragrance of mimeograph ink as I performed my part of the printing process. I turned the big handle on the end of the press at a steady pace around and around and around. The arithmetic homework papers printed perfectly. Mrs. Baxa was pleased. I was gleeful. All too soon the copies had been printed. Now for cookies and milk that Mrs. Baxa hoped would not spoil my supper.

She thanked me with a big smile and the encouragement that I was a fine young man. On the climb up our hill toward home, I felt taller and my head was filled with thoughts of love. Or was it the mimeograph ink?

THE BLUE AND GRAY GARDEN

Our roots in Upshur County go back to the Revolutionary War with the Pringle brothers and Bush's Fort. But the Civil War shed Upshur blood, too. In the third grade at Academy Grade School, Miss Swisher thrilled our class with her stories of the battle for Buckhannon. She showed us shot dug from her garden on Boggess Street. Every spring she'd dig up more. The battle had raged right on her property. As she told us, I could picture the gray forces holding the hill beside City Park where I would grow up. The blue forces held the hill where Dad would practice medicine in the old Barlow Home/St. Joseph's Hospital. Miss Swisher's garden was a war chest, a treasure trove. So when she asked for volunteers to run down to her residence and get her Civil War booty bag for her class presentation, I waved my hand the highest. Choose me! Please! Please! Please!

"OK, Greenbrier, you go directly to my home. The front door is unlocked. My bag is just inside in the foyer on the left next to my gun case. Pick it up. Return quickly. Don't dilly-dally."

Off I ran like greased lightning. Everything was just like Miss Swisher told me. I guess she had been too excited about her presentation and just left it in the morning when she walked to school.

As I ran back, I remembered an earlier time when Miss Swisher let me run an errand to take a folded-up message to her good friend and teacher at Buckhannon High School. Miss Beth Darnell taught in a science class in the basement of the old building. I was directed to run down from Academy Grade School across the baseball outfield. There was a side entrance to the high school with massive stone steps. Up I ran, skipping steps. For a third grader, the doors proved massive, but I was strong. I ran up to the office where Principal Newt Anderson met me and allowed me to go back to the basement to give "Miss Beth" her message.

My reverie over, I returned to Miss Swisher's class. This time she reached in her bag and gave me a reward. Wow! Civil War shot! I knew for sure that in the spring, I would ask Mom and Dad to let me weed the garden.

A MOST WONDERFUL DAY

Happiness comes to us one percent here, three percent there. Rarely are there 100 percent happy days. I've had a few. What a wonderful day my wife of now 36 years and I celebrated at EvUnBreth Acres on our wedding day. What a tremendous day I shared with my sisters and mom and dad when I graduated from the West Virginia University School of Medicine. Glory!

And what a wonderful day when they tore down my grade school!!! I knew it was coming. Our summer baseball league coach, Frank Feola, told us so. He said the old section of the old Academy Grade School would come crashing down into center field the following day. We would not play ball, but we could come and watch a bulldozer attached to a heavy chain linked through the ground floor windows of my third-grade classroom give a heave. We loved to play tug-of-war on the sandy playground. This would be a giant tug-of-war between the bulldozer and the Academy School.

Dad told me that I'd need my red cowboy bandana to cover my mouth, as there would be a large cloud of dust. Wow! Mom prepared my lunch of peanut butter and strawberry jam sandwiches, knowing that I would be watching from early morning until the school was destroyed. There would be no leaving the site until I had witnessed my dream come true. At the end of every school year we sang, "School's out! School's out! The teacher let the mules out!" My relationship with school was definitely a love/hate affair.

I saddled up our horse Pinto Scout and called to Brier, my collie dog. We would go together to share the most fun we had ever had!!! All summer we were inseparable. Usually we'd head for Mount Hibbs, and then on over to Leonard Holler, where we could build tree houses and dam up the stream.

Coach Feola said we should stay behind the backstop to be safe from flying debris. It certainly took a long time to get the chain in place and the bulldozer squared away. If they would have let my friend Danny Bennett drive, it would have been over quickly. Danny drove all over his parents' farm out on Hickory Flat, although he was only ten years old like me. Even Ricky Summers would make short work of the destruction. He drove a tractor with his granddad out on their Brushy Fork farm. These adults are just too slow, I decided. They should let us kids pull down our own school!

Finally, the moment we all anticipated arrived. The old part of the Academy had housed the first part of what we knew as West Virginia Wesleyan College, now on a campus further down College Avenue. It was a really old, old, old building with five-brick thick walls. The bulldozer pulled. The Academy pulled back.

Back and forth.
Tension and release.
Creaking and groaning.

Then there was a crack down from Miss Hall's room to Miss Swisher's room below. Then a bigger crack from Miss Cookman's room to Miss Swisher's room. The groan grew louder. The building sounded alive. It was like a dragon or dinosaur lived inside and had been wounded. Suddenly, the tumult crescendoed. Brier barked. Pinto Scout reared up in surprise. I laughed with my friends until we fell down ourselves, unable to contain our happiness. We rolled around, throwing dust in the air. We laughed some more. Truly, a most wonderful day!!!

PEPTO-BISMOL BLUE

"Pepto-Bismol blue" has become a very important color in my life. This is not because I have had a great need for the pink-colored soothing medicine. Rather, my life has been immeasurably impacted by the cobalt blue color, which was the trademark color for Pepto-Bismol bottles back in the late 1950s when I was 11 years old. Today, Ebay has a pair of antique cobalt blue Pepto-Bismol bottles listed for $636. However, my memories involving the color are priceless.

First there was the demolishing of our Academy Grade School, requiring us to attend fifth grade at the EvUnBreth Acres Church Camp. In particular, Miss Edith Hall's class met in the "Pepto-Bismol blue" chapel. The large chapel had three-story-tall cobalt blue windows on both sides of the sanctuary. How cool and soothing the room felt. Any hyperactive kids in the fifth grade were turned from lion cubs to kitty cats. Being in a church demanded a certain decorum, according to Miss Hall. We could sing spirituals, showing respect for our surroundings. "Swing Low, Sweet Chariot" led me to imagine a cobalt blue Jordan River.

Even our reading selections were impacted by the chapel classroom. The stories of the Blue and Gray Civil War came alive with Miss Hall's telling. We memorized the Gettysburg Address. We even hiked as a class to Twin Rock Peak, overlooking the church camp. On a blue sky day, Miss Hall taught us that the Battle of Buckhannon was fought in the wide valley stretching before us. The Revolutionary War also became living history from the mountain top. On one side we could see the Pringle Tree growing on the banks of the blue waters of the Buckhannon River. The tree was home for John and Samuel Pringle when they were hiding from the British troops and from the local Indian tribes. On the other side we could see Ivanhoe upstream, where the Pringles were buried. Later we hiked to the giant sycamore tree to see how many kids we could pack into the hollow trunk.

All too soon, fifth grade passed. But the heavenly cobalt blue chapel stayed imprinted in my mind as holy ground. So naturally, "Pepto-Bismol blue" came to mind when I proposed marriage to Araceli as we basked in the sun on a rock in the middle of the Greenbrier River just below the Blue Stone Dam. What a wonderful Labor Day weekend to pledge love to one another. The following year, on September 13, 1975, we gathered in the presence of family and friends as witnesses in the presence of God, with sun streaming through the cobalt blue windows of the chapel at EvUnBreth Acres. Just as in the fifth grade, I felt peaceful and serene in the blue chapel. "I will," we promised each other. Two young doctors promising true love in a chapel the color of a medicine bottle. Ironic really, but fitting, given the importance of this setting in my growth and development.

More than 36 years later, the white clouds and the blue sky are filled once more in my mind's eye with the loving white doves Araceli and I released from giant Filipino baskets that day. Perfectly in sync with our union, a pair of love birds flew around our blue water lakeside wedding reception, approving our pledge of love. Then the flock of doves circled our cobalt blue-windowed chapel. They were as white as the chapel walls, dancing in and out of view just as my childhood memories danced around.

NINETY-NINE TIMES
OUT OF A HUNDRED

Betty Hicks, my sixth-grade teacher, loved to assert that certain things were factual and actual by proclaiming "ninety-nine times out of a hundred..." That I remember her saying this does not mean that I was turning into a sassy teenager when I was her student. No, it's just that I questioned how precise she could actually be. However, one thing *is* certain: attending sixth grade in a two-room schoolhouse proved to be one of the best years of my education.

Paul Mearns and Betty Hicks taught the sixth-grade classes for the Academy Grade School the year after our school was condemned, torn down, and in the process of being rebuilt. Students were farmed out all over town. The old Tennerton Grade School might have been on its last legs, but it would do just fine for us. There was a lot of "making due" that year, but from my perspective, it was a wonderful time.

Hot lunch was cooked in the hallway, as Miss Phillips, our cook, had no other kitchen. I still marvel at the hot rolls and other tempting treats she cooked up for us. In fact, I bragged on her so much that my cousin, Kirk Treible, hired her to cook for the Phi Sigma Epsilon Fraternity the following year when he became a senior at West Virginia Wesleyan College and president of his fraternity.

Outdoor privies served us well, with the girls having their outhouse in left field and the boys having theirs in center field. Playing on our baseball field required the use of the back of the school for a backstop behind home plate. If we hit a home run, it was up against a hill that served us well for sleigh riding in winter. Yes, we brought our sleds to school but also used metal Coke signs as flying saucers.

Nora Amundsen came to teach us French. She also enlarged our worldview, telling us how she lived on soup all winter to save money to travel in Russia and Iran during the summers. We affectionately called her "Amazon," as she had the stature of a basketball player. She was quite a teacher, not afraid to yell at us "fermez la bouche," the French version of "shut up."

Recess offered us a chance to dance boys with girls. Rock 'n' roll was young and we wanted to be hip. "Puppy love" took on a new meaning for me. Previously, my affections were reserved for Brier Boy, our family dog. Now it was extended to secret crushes.

Even the bus ride home from our wooden schoolhouse proved fun. We had a great "excuse me, ma'am" when the bus would sharply turn off Kanawha Street to Barbour Street. The prize seating was at the back of the bus, allowing us to go airborne when we came to the bump in the road.

Yes, Mrs. Hicks, I am "ninety-nine times out of a hundred" certain that we grew up in a golden era and in an age of innocence.

HOOK, LINE, AND SINKER

Elizabeth Curry, my ninth-grade English teacher at Buckhannon-Upshur Junior High School, may not have known much about fishing in the Buckhannon River beside her home, but she did know a lot about how to catch her students' previously unrealized love for literature. She made an offer to Bill Anderson, George Lulos, and me that we could not refuse. Her proposition was quite simple: "Young men, come over to my home this Thursday, and I will serve up a delicious strawberry milkshake for each of you. We will enjoy the rich, creamy, fruit-filled food of the gods for an hour or so as you tell me about a book that you have read in the past week."

We were so excited that we talked of nothing else all week. Free strawberry milkshakes just for reading a book! Our mouths drooled. The walk along Island Avenue shortened its normal time by half as we hurried to Mrs. Curry's. True to her promise, she offered one of the best shakes I've ever enjoyed. And refills.

We talked of *Moby Dick*, *White Fang* and *Treasure Island*. The discussion even proved fun. Mrs. Curry listened, nodded, probed, and encouraged. "Let's do it again next week, fellows! What about chocolate milkshakes?"

Wild horses could not keep us away the next week. We read on. *Green Mansions*. *Old Man and the Sea*. *Black Beauty*. And Mrs. Curry offered seconds on double chocolate shakes with whipped cream.

Week after week, Bill, George, and I anticipated with glee our time at Mrs. Curry's home. "Iron sharpens iron," she declared, as we now questioned each other about what our authors wanted to say with their novels. We questioned the accuracy of the descriptive details. We probed why one story became a classic and another a dud. By the end of the ninth grade, we proved a worthy catch.

Bill Anderson went on to become our Class of 1966 Valedictorian. George Lulos became our Class of 1966 Salutatorian. I went on to read the 100 greatest books ever written, scoring in the 99th percentile on the Medical College Acceptance Test and gaining early acceptance to the West Virginia University School of Medicine. Mrs. Curry, thank you from here to eternity for catching us hook, line, and sinker!

Euarctos
americanus

WEST VIRGINIA

State Animal

EXPANDING HORIZONS

TAP DANCING ABOVE
THE FIVE AND DIME

Tap dancing had a certain appeal to me. For one thing, I got a new pair of patent leather shoes that had metal taps on the heels and toes. I loved making my feet a percussive instrument. Clicking and clacking all over the hardwood floor made a great deal of racket. What glee! What fun! What sheer joy!

Another variety of tap dancing was the Irish sidestep that my Grandparents Flanagan enjoyed. Something in their Irish past was awakened when I stepped back and forth like Bob Hope or Shirley Temple. They had a black and white television, around which we would gather for special shows and on many Saturday mornings. I loved my grandparents and would do almost anything to please them. Certainly I liked improvisation as we formed flying circles with arms swinging as well as tapping. All that jazz, pretending that I was in Vaudeville, made me happy.

Heel and toe
Heel and toe
Slide, slide, slide

The syncopated rhythm proved to be my favorite part of tap dancing. In my mind, I was that little train engine climbing the mountain.

I think I can.
I think I can.
I think I can.

Given all that I liked about tap dancing, maybe I could have graduated from Bill DeFare's School of Dance above the Murphy's Five and Dime to a Broadway career, except for one simple fact. I was eight years old, and girls were already a sore spot in my life. Not that I did not love my sisters, but they always wanted to play with the boys and we did not want them around most of the time. Well, our dance class was filled with girls! In fact, there were only two other boys. My, my. We felt sorry for ourselves.

My dance career ended the day the two Mackey girls kissed me. One kissed me on the left cheek. The other kissed me on the right cheek. They had ganged up on me! A team of wild horses could not drag me back to the dance school after that.

SLIPHORNS

Standing tall in front of the Buckhannon-Upshur Junior High band, Dave Reemsnyder, Jake Huffman, and I felt that anticipatory anxiety necessary for a great performance. Dick Lawson, our band director, entrusted his trombone trio with the top billing for our winter concert. Mr. Lawson thanked all the parents, as well as relatives and friends, for braving the snowstorm to come out on a blustery evening. He told them that they would not be disappointed.

Tapping the music stand in front of him with his director's baton, Mr. Lawson caught the attention of all the band members, who snapped their instruments into their "go" positions. He looked around at us and smiled, then peered over the sections of the band, studying their readiness before lifting his baton, finally signaling with a dramatic downbeat. Dave, Jake, and I loved our instruments. We particularly loved this song "Oh, Dem Golden Sliphorns," an arrangement of the 1940s band tune "Oh, Dem Golden Slippers," featuring trombones. The trombones are meant to slide from position one all the way to position seven with grace and dignity. Then, in a naughty sort of way, trombones slide clear back from seven to one. We were playing in perfect harmony on three octaves. Finally my solo came. Starting with a high C and pressing my lips against my mouthpiece. I climbed two more octaves slipping and sliding ad lib, Dixieland style. Glory!

The applause was thunderous in the echoing old B-UHS gym. Mr. Lawson never liked the acoustics for band performances. He said a glossy paint job can ruin a room. But tonight, the echo just made the appreciation of our audience all the more real. In the final bow before we returned to the trombone section, I reflected on the hard work that had paid off. Every day I'd take my horn home for a half-hour practice. After fracturing my fibula in a freak bike accident, speeding in our basement, my extra climbing of our hill with a heavy walking cast had scored big. I had the lung power necessary to really belt it out.

In a final flight of fantasy, I imagined Cinderella's slipper as a golden slipper. Someday, I'd serenade my true love; I'd hit high C.

BUCKHANNON GRADE SCHOOL TIMES

Early on I learned to follow some of my classmates who were natural leaders. Steve Brown was one of those. So in the fifth grade, when Steve proposed that he publish and I edit a newspaper, I readily said yes.

We could see an emerging news market, as East Main Street School, Central School, Academy School, and Tennerton School all came together for Saturday basketball games at the Buckhannon-Upshur Junior High School gym. We really did not know each other very well, but someday we would all be Buccaneers together once we got to high school. Often we would come at 8 am when the gym opened and stay all day, watching all the teams play and just hanging out. Our own game might be at 11 am, but we did not want to miss any of the action.

Undertaking our newspaper, we made big plans. Even our masthead had the famous slogan taken from the *New York Times:* "All the news that's fit to print." We had game scores with stats. We had interest columns covering such topics as opinions on the question, "What would you do if someone told you your epidermis is showing?" We had lovelorn columns as crushes came and went. In short, everything was fit to print.

Grandmother Flanagan showed me how to take a potato and carve it to form a letter or a figure. Then it could be pressed into an ink blotter and pressed onto the newspaper page to make an illustration. Dad told me of how he had written messages on birch bark when hiking the Appalachian Trail. We figured we might try that but never did. Apparently, postage could be applied to the bark and the US Postal Service would accept and deliver it. Steve vetoed my idea of doing what the *Hillbilly*, a weekly newspaper, did for one spring edition. They printed their paper with ramp juice ink, which really smelled up the post office as well as folks' homes. Steve always did show good judgment beyond our years.

Our *Buckhannon Grade School Times* laid a firm foundation for us. We proved to ourselves that we could accomplish anything we set our minds to do. Years later, Steve became the president of the Buckhannon-Upshur Class of 1966. Now that is news that is fit to print!

ANOTHER TIME AND ANOTHER PLACE

"The sun rises and the sun sets on Buckhannon-Upshur High School," Mike Adams said as we prepared for another long summer band practice. Saul Fisher, our band director, knew we needed to be ready for the Southeastern United States Band Festival in Virginia Beach, Virginia in mid-June. Mike meant to complain about our marching band practice, but I could see another meaning besides.

We were part of something really important. Soon we would be representing not only our school, but also our community and our state when we performed concert band and marching band shows. For a year, we had been working on some pretty tough classical music with Dick Lawson, our junior high band director. He had confidence in us. Most of us attended the West Virginia Wesleyan Summer Band Camp just to hone our skills. Dr. Buell Agey and Dr. Bobbi Loftis gave us private lessons as well as sectional lessons. I felt totally devoted to our B-U Band.

We were on the road at last. What fun, singing about "ninety-nine bottles of beer" and counting clear down to one. What anticipation of excellence in performance! We joked that after we blew the competition away, literally, with our horn playing, West Virginia would have the respect we deserve. We were up against schools from Florida and even Texas. Mr. Fisher, a lifelong bachelor, probably was over his head with more than 140 children, but he remained cool and calm. Just seeing the Atlantic Ocean proved overwhelming to us mountaineers. We got back to being barefoot in a hurry.

After more practices, we performed, earning "Superior" in concert performance and taking home an album cut from our great band sound. However, we were disappointed in our field competition when our choreographed spinning wheels spun out of control. The sound remained great, which is important for a band, but we all felt we let Mr. Fisher down. He remained equanimous.

What happened next makes me sure that I now live in a different time and a far different country. Saul Fisher and my mom and dad agreed that I could get off the B-U Band bus in Richmond, Virginia. There I'd catch a bus to Philadelphia, Pennsylvania, where I'd transfer to another bus to Atlantic City, New Jersey, finally meeting up with my family. They would be vacationing while my dad participated in continuing medical education courses with the American Medical Association Convention. Spending all night in the bus station in Philadelphia would be out of the question for our children or our grandchildren now. However, in 1963 as a 15-year-old, I felt no fear, nor was I approached by anybody wishing to sell me dope or do me harm. The weirdest thing that happened was that I played pinball machines all night to stay awake and pass the time. I came to find out that the pinball machines at the Spudnut Shop across from B-U High School were better than the ones in the big city bus station. The balls in the machines in Upshur County were steel balls with a lot of play in each bounce, while the Philly bus station games had wooden balls which were too light to really wrack up game-winning points.

I also discovered that there is no place like home.

ARTIFICIAL RECITATION

Looking back, perhaps my early impression was wrong. As a youngster, I felt that the Woman's Christian Temperance Union did not go about indoctrinating us very well. I did know these silver-haired ladies were most determined. Many had been born before women's suffrage. Gaining the right to vote had emboldened them to get a United States Constitutional Amendment for the prohibition of alcohol. Yes, they were strong women.

The WCTU sponsored the Loyal Temperance League and the Youth Temperance Council. Starting at a young age, I recall going to meetings where we recited the Pledge to the American Flag and the Pledge to the Christian Flag. Then we pledged not to let tobacco nor alcohol touch our lips. We sang simple songs with much repetition about the evils of tobacco and alcohol. We did activities like coloring and pasting to make posters for placement in downtown Buckhannon stores about the evils of substance abuse.

But I felt we were not really being impacted by the message. It felt like it was in one ear and out the other. I did have a simple version of the WCTU message: "I don't drink and I don't chew, and I don't go with girls who do!" Maybe I was impacted some.

In the fifth grade, I was encouraged to enter a speech contest. The requirement was simple. Memorize a five-paragraph talk and present to a panel of the silver-haired ladies. I did not like to speak in public, but the prize was a trip to Charleston, West Virginia, with an overnight at the Daniel Boone Hotel. Now there was a hero, Daniel Boone! How could I resist? I did my best, and I won. Really, I do not remember what I said, but they arranged for me to give the talk on the local WBUC radio station. And we had a great time at the Daniel Boone.

Lo and behold, I won the West Virginia state contest, so the silver-haired ladies and I traveled to Columbus, Ohio for the United States regional contest. The hotel sure was swanky. The strange part for me was the flat land. You cannot get above the trees and look down on the countryside in Ohio. I had to learn another talk for the regional meeting, which I memorized and recited, but not as well. I failed to progress to the next level, but I was pleased to have made it that far.

My clique of friends all had promised not to smoke, to chew, or to drink alcohol. We gave our pledge. We "crossed our heart and hoped to die" if we violated our oath. As the drug culture of the 1960s emerged, I was determined to keep my word.

So thank you, silver-haired ladies of the WCTU, for encouraging what I felt was just artificial recitation. Looks like the process worked, just like artificial resuscitation, which is life saving in many instances.

HIS FACE SHINING

The LORD bless thee, and keep thee:
The LORD make his face shine upon thee,
and be gracious unto thee:
The LORD lift up his countenance upon thee,
and give thee peace.

-Numbers 6:24-26

Living beyond Buckhannon City Park sheltered us. The park provided a mantel of dark, keeping our night sky perfectly black for stargazing in the backyard on summer evenings. It minimized light pollution from the street lights of our small mountain village. I grew to love the new moon nights. The darker, the better.

Only when youth activities drew me away after dark from our hilltop home did I get to appreciate how black was the walk under the canopy of our forested park. Sundays after Methodist Youth Fellowship, I'd hike through the park singing our MYF song, "The Lord bless you and keep you...." I learned that Jesus called me to be light and salt. In creation God said, "Let there be light." One MYF meditation on Shekinah Glory, teaching us about God's Glorious Presence, changed my perception of dark forever.

"Mom, how can the bush burn but not be consumed?" I inquired of my mother upon reading the Bible account of Moses' encounter with God in the burning bush. She told me of her experience in her student days, with a ball of lightning bouncing down the sidewalk toward her in front of the West Virginia Wesleyan College Administration Building. Her instant prayer to God was "to bless me and keep me." Lo and behold, the giant ball of lightning bounced over her, causing her to feel the heat and be blinded by the light but remain unharmed. She knew God was gracious to her.

"Dad, how can a pillar of cloud by day and a pillar of light by night guide Moses and the Israelites for 40 years?" I inquired of my father. He told me of the Aurora Borealis often observed along the northern reaches of the Appalachian Trail. Electrically charged oxygen and nitrogen provide a wonderful light show on the darkest nights. God taught Dad to study carefully the pale green, blue, and violet Northern Lights dancing overhead. The power of observation is important for a doctor to have, Dad pointed out. Sometimes a life is saved through keen observations, honed in the darkest night.

"What about the Glory of the Lord shining on the shepherds the night Jesus was born?" I asked Grandfather Flanagan. He described the Triune nature of God, just like water, ice, and steam: God, the Father; God, the Son; God, the Holy Spirit. That first Christmas night, Glory came down. Grandfather challenged me the next time that I came home after dark, walking from the First Methodist Church through the Buckhannon City Park, to pray to God and ask for Shekinah Glory to light my path.

I could hardly wait for the next new moon Sunday evening to experience God's light, whether it would be a ball of lightning, the Aurora Borealis, or the Glory of the Lord! As I entered the park, leaving the street lights of Park Street behind, I began to sing, "The Lord bless me and keep me, the Lord make His face to shine upon me. . . ." Surprisingly, my eyes adapted to the dark like our cat, "Dick Ralston." I could see the outlines of the trees and the roots making the path uneven. I heard the whippoorwill sing and I whistled back. I felt a peace that passed all understanding. In my heart, I knew God's face was shining down.

THE THOUSAND-YARD STARE

Younger 4-H Camp is often a time for homesickness, as for many of us, this is our first time away from home. But I determined to be brave. Separation anxiety had come to me earlier, when we moved from our garage home to our new home just next door on Valentine's Day when I was in the second grade. Mom and Dad had prepared me well, but by habit I had rushed into the old living room, and the walls and floor and room were totally bare. Shocked, I could hardly catch my breath. My cry echoed around the car bay of the garage, making all surreal. But it was momentary when I realized we had at last moved to our new home that had been under construction for more than a year. My anxiety was over in a minute, but Mom and Dad explained that some children are homeless, or do not have food to eat, or even are not safe from the adults in their lives, but are neglected and abused.

As a doctor, my dad depended on clinical history and physical examination to reach a diagnosis even for anxiety. He told me of the "thousand-yard stare" that he saw so often when he was one of two doctors with General Douglas MacArthur in WWII and the Occupation of Japan.

Younger 4-H Camp in Selbyville went well, and I became a true Delaware Indian brave. I played volleyball on our winning team, beating the socks off the other tribes. I sang loudly and said "how how" often. And yet I was hardly prepared for what happened during the Sadie Hawkins party on Thursday evening, the last night of camp. A dark-haired Indian maiden of another tribe approached me and said, "Ladies' choice."

"Who, me?" I replied, as I heard her words but could see that she was not looking directly at me. Though I'd never seen a "thousand-yard stare" before, now I had. She seemed lost in time and space, but was indeed standing there asking me to dance.

Now I was glad I had joined my classmate Sherry for her tenth birthday party in her home on Kanawha Hill, when her mom had taught me to dance. She had positioned my arms just right and told me to imagine a box on the floor. Step to the right. Step back. Step to the left. Step forward. Turn around. "See, dancing is easy," her mom had explained. Indeed, I got the knack of it. 4-H Camp provided yet another opportunity to grow. I said yes to the Indian maiden with the "thousand-yard stare." We stepped onto the crowded dance floor in the Assembly Hall as Paul Anka began to sing his hit song, "Put Your Head On My Shoulder."

The dance was over all too soon for me. I enjoyed it, really. We talked for a moment as we more formally introduced ourselves. I was from town. She was from the country. I had four sisters. She was a foster child and had no family. She had already lived in five foster homes. We both had "West Virginia Trees" 4-H projects. Maybe we would see each other at the Upshur County Fall 4-H Exhibit. "Thank you very much," we both declared. At the time of the Fall Exhibit, the Indian maiden was missing in action. She had been moved to another foster home, and the report was that she had been abused.

Turn around.

The Indian maiden is in a countywide talent show and wins singing the song "Put Your Head On My Shoulder."

Turn around.

The Indian maiden is growing grotesquely obese as I see her in the Buckhannon-Upshur Junior High hallways.

Turn around.

The report is that she is pregnant and dropping out of school.

Turn around.

Now the report is that the Indian maiden's fiancé is abusive, and her children are removed from her home to foster care.

Turn around.

The obituary announces the unexpected death of the Indian maiden at 33 years of age.

Turn around.

This Indian brave practices psychiatric medicine, often treating Post-Traumatic Stress Disorder in children who have a "thousand-yard stare."

Rhododendron maximum

WEST VIRGINIA State Flower

UPSHUR COUNTY

SPLIT ROCK

"Dad, why do you make house calls?" I asked my father one day as we drove in his green Jeep out toward Sago to see a sick child.

"First, I really learn a lot about how my patients live when I visit their homes. Staying healthy is as important as getting healthy. 'An ounce of prevention is worth a pound of cure,'" Dad taught. "You see hardworking people striving to improve, and you see lazy bones. Second, many of my patients are poor and do not even have a ride into town to visit our office," he explained.

I knew he was proud of his new office. Aunt Julia and Uncle Walter and their family built the office in 1958, just the previous year, when Mom was pregnant with Bethie, my youngest sister. Dad went on, "Keep your eyes peeled today and tell me what you learn from our house call."

We drove on past Sago until the road changed from asphalt to gravel. Then we climbed a hill that was green with summer oak, poplar, and maple trees overshadowing the country lane. At a gate on the right side of the road, we stopped to let ourselves in, carefully closing it behind us to keep the cows grazing in the meadow from getting the itch to see if the grass was greener on the other side. Now the road was grassy and bumpy with red bone. Dad explained that the family burned coal mined from the exposed coal seam behind their house. Red bone is the hard ash and rock left over. After a country mile, we came to a second gate which we opened and closed as before. Now the farmhouse was spotted. It was handmade from leftover sawmill slabs, as larger logs were squared and prepared for cutting into lumber. Some places the slabs were covered with tar paper, but some with old Sunday school lessons pasted over the cracks in the irregular slabs.

Next we opened a garden gate that closed automatically due to a horseshoe weight. Inside, climbing the stick fence topped off with mason jars, roses bloomed as well as sweet peas. Dad said the lady of the house ruled the roost. We climbed up the rock steps—just stones gathered off the hillside and strategically placed, no concrete needed. The cowbell near the door called the farmer and their kids in for meals, Dad noted. He let me ring the bell loudly. Inside, the room was dark with the shades pulled. The sickbed was by the Burnside stove and near a fireplace to the right. A big rocker was occupied by the mother holding a little girl in her arms, wrapped in a handmade quilt. The creak of the rocker on the uneven floor boards was noticeable. I liked the rhythm; it was like a clock ticking.

"Mommy can hold you, honey," said Dad as he set his doctor bag on the bedside and opened it up to find his thermometer. He kept it in an alcohol-filled glass tube. He shook off the alcohol before slipping it into the little girl's mouth, asking her to close down on it gently as he placed it under her tongue. Carefully he checked head, ears, eyes, nose, and throat. Then he drew out his stethoscope to check the chest and listen to the belly, followed by gentle palpation. The mom had a furrow in her brow as deep as a furrow plowed in a garden.

Dad drew up to a full sitting position, preparing to make a pronouncement. He liked to teach. "You called me just in time, for your daughter has 'P---neumonia.'" He emphasized the "P" which is silent in the medical term. "Fortunately it has not spread to the heart, and we can treat it with a shot of penicillin." For follow-up he advised the family to walk down the hill to the railroad tracks the following week and flag down the coal train from Pickens. "Bring her to Buckhannon to my new office, which is at 27 South Kanawha Street. It will cost a quarter both ways, but I want her to come to the office to check her urine, as streptococcus can infect the kidney, and I want to make sure her lungs are clear."

He turned to the father standing by and asked if he'd

take us up to Split Rock, further up the holler. Other brothers and sisters seemed to appear from the woodwork. We all trooped up together to the rock formation Dad had heard about. Like discovering Sleeping Beauty's castle, I could not have been more thrilled when I spied the 50-foot-high rock formation covering several acres. In the middle was a giant split about 3 feet wide at the bottom that beckoned us into the heart of the sandstone formation. As we squeezed our way into the heart of stone, I felt chilled. Ice from the previous winter covered the rocky floor. The farmer's children led the way, proud to live by such a famous "Natural Wonder of Upshur County," as Doc described.

On the far side, the farmer showed us his beehives, drawing out several cones of "honey," as Dad had called his daughter. He asked Doc if he would accept these in payment and Dad agreed. "Lois told me we are low on honey. Thank you very much."

All too soon, Dad and I were hiking out of Split Rock holler. "Well, Greenbrier, what did you learn today by keeping your eyes peeled?" Dad queried.

"That I want to grow up to be a doctor like you, Dad!" I exclaimed.

WAGON WHEEL CAVE

"Doctors must be curious," Dad plainly asserted. "Doctors make the diagnosis from a whole range of possible diagnoses called differential diagnoses," he explained in earnest. "Today you will see something that I cannot explain."

Dad and I hiked down a logging road toward one of the "Seven Wonders of Upshur County." He and I had a project together for the county-wide 4-H Speech and Demonstration Contest. Our destination was Wagon Wheel Cave. Upshurites needed to be educated about our county's unique features. Moonshiners found this hidden rock formation perfect for boiling brew. There was a circular rock the size of a football field, shaped perfectly like a wagon wheel with a hole in the middle. It looked like it had slipped off a giant chariot, landing partly embedded in the mountain stream near Mount Etna. The hole provided a chimney for the smoke of a hardwood fire, while the area under the rock provided protection for the moonshine still out of the weather and out of sight.

As we climbed over fallen trees strewn across the road, Dad explained the mystery of phosphorescence. Normally in nature, where there is smoke there is fire. To have fire, three things are required: fuel, heat, and oxygen. But here at the Wagon Wheel Cave there is "cool light" on the ceiling. Dad got more excited. Cool light is what lightning bugs have. That blinking light covering our yards and meadows provided endless hours of summer fun catching lightning bugs and storing them in our mason jars. What causes cool emission light would make the discoverer the next Thomas Edison.

As we hiked, I began to feel that Dad wanted me to be that inventor/scientist. "The truth lies at the Wagon Wheel Cave," Dad declared. Maybe aliens from outer space have landed here and set up a base camp. They are further advanced than mere human mortals. They have discovered low energy lighting. That was my contribution to the differential diagnosis. Dad did not discount it entirely, but he shook his head no.

Finally arriving at the Wagon Wheel Cave, Dad did concede that a previous exposure to x-rays or another energy source could be part of the mystery. After that source is removed, the light persists. "Maybe the potent corn whiskey is evaporating onto the roof of the cave, creating a chemical reaction of oxidation," he theorized. Dad instructed me to take a rock from the floor of the cave and scratch the ceiling. I stretched up and scribbled my name. It was amazing to see "GREENBRIER" in a blue light just as if I'd written in chalk across a blackboard. Dad wrote, "DOC LOVES SUGAR PLUM." We laughed at ourselves. Both boys! Both doctors!

PRINGLE TREE, A NATURAL WONDER

Sycamore trees, or as my biologist mother would call them, "Platanus Occidentalis," are known to have the largest trunk diameters of any of the eastern American hardwoods. So it is no surprise that the early history of Upshur County is so entwined with this giant of our West Virginia forests. Also, it is no surprise that Dad and Mom suggested that our list of the "Seven Natural Wonders of Upshur County" include our majestic Pringle Tree, our giant sycamore growing for over a hundred years on the banks of the Buckhannon River.

Even my grandmother, Mary Barnes Flanagan, got excited about the choice. As a deaconess in Richwood, West Virginia, the hardwood capital of the world, prior to her marriage to the Reverend Paul L. Flanagan, she had come to love the deep, cool shade of the sycamore. She liked the tree's characteristic of sending out large horizontal branches just a few feet up the trunk. Her telling of the Biblical story of curious Zaccheus who climbed a sycamore tree to spy Jesus on his triumphal entry into Jerusalem made me curious to climb our Pringle Tree, too.

Her stories of the prophet Amos, herdsman and dresser of sycamores, gave me ideas of defending truth and justice. I could picture Amos as an Old Testament Superman who likewise would defend truth and justice and the American way on Grandmother's black and white television.

Even the trunk of our Pringle Tree had the military camouflage pattern that inspired my imagination. I could play Amos/Superman, pretending to be dressed in military garb. Grandmother loved to have me dramatize a Scripture passage and encouraged me to be a pastor someday. How I loved to proclaim, "But let judgment run down as waters, and righteousness as a mighty stream," quoting Amos 5:24.

Even before Dad and Mom helped with my 4-H project, my grandparents and Uncle Paul took us out for picnics at the Pringle Tree. Our current sycamore was believed to be the third one at that site, but was nearly as grand as the original tree that housed John and Samuel Pringle when they took absence without leave from Fort Pitt and the British Forces encamped there. Coming by canoe upstream, they fortunately found a giant sycamore to winter in. Fence rails are traditionally 11 feet long. The brothers wrote in their journals that they could stand in the middle of the hollow sycamore with a fence rail and turn completely around. This would mean the diameter was more than 22 feet. When Uncle Paul helped me step off the diameter of the current sycamore "living room," I found it to be about 11 feet across. The brothers each had bedrooms up in the hollow horizontal branches about 6 feet off the floor of the hollow room. Even today the horizontal branches are continuing to hollow out.

When I gave my 4-H speech and came to the telling of the Pringle Tree as one of our "Seven Natural Wonders," I noticed that the younger kids were most curious to visit our giant sycamore and climb up the outside and the inside. Truly, we are blessed to have our giant sycamore growing on the banks of the Buckhannon River.

SHORTCUT TO SPRUCE FALLS

Spruce Falls made Doc's cut for the "Seven Natural Wonders of Upshur County" list. The 50-foot drop into a rocky pool viewed from the top of a canyon wall makes the sight mystical and magical. The thick spruce and hemlock canopy darkens and cools the stream even on the hottest summer day. And there are plenty of rocks to climb on. This is truly a hide-and-go-seek paradise.

Dad had criteria for the "Seven Natural Wonders" that harkened back to his days of helping construct and then hiking the Appalachian Trail. The sight must beckon you. It must draw you to the very edge of the rim. The mist rising must inspire the imagination. Peer closely. Are there bobcats lurking? Is that an eagle's nest? Spy any brown trout swimming?

Since Spruce Falls was only five miles from our home as the crow flies, Dale Berisford, Brian Shreve (who lived only a stone's throw from the Falls), and dozens of Boy Scouts from Troop 128 enjoyed the ten-mile, First Class hike to and from the Falls. Up until the day of the encounter with danger, I could talk any of my friends or fellow Scouts into taking a shortcut. After the encounter, nobody wanted to hear about shortcuts.

That day took on lasting significance of Biblical proportions: BC—before confrontation; AD—after danger. Ten Scouts left the First United Methodist Church, Boy Scout headquarters for Troop 128, bright and early that fall day. We climbed through the City Park and hiked to the top of Mount Hibbs. Compass in hand, we headed straight for Spruce Falls due west. This was through a horse pasture where a dozen stallions and mares watched us with cautious interest. Next we strolled along a recently cut pasture and to the top of a forested ridge where the high tension wires crossed. I walked slightly ahead since this was my shortcut.

Soon we were on the Summers' Farm. We paused at a fishing pond to throw rocks. There we also remembered our friend Ricky Summers, who had tragically died a few short years earlier when he fell from the hay wagon his grandfather was pulling. Ricky had always been the strongest of the Scouts. He had held on to the wagon even after his fall. Unfortunately, his elderly grandfather did not hear his calls. And just as unfortunately, Ricky did not let go. So he was dragged some distance, sustaining traumatic brain injury followed by a coma from which he did not awaken.

Shaken by the remembrance, we reflected upon the Scout's Honor: "I will do my duty to God and Country." Pat Nickell, our Scoutmaster, weekly emphasized that "a Scout is reverent." Our minister, Rossing Smith, spoke at our Second Class Court of Honor, reminding us to form lifelong healthy habits. He told us that life is a journey down a road that will have trials and troubles which he likened to ruts. "Pick your rut; you will be in it for a lifetime!" he preached. We felt that day that God was blessing our rutted road.

The next hill climbed and fence crossed, we caught a glimpse of Dr. Basil Page's farm. Our classmate, Guylow Williams, would be expecting us. We planned to refill our canteens from her well. She also promised apple pie if we were hungry. But before we could go on further, something happened. A tall, muscular farmer stepped from behind a tree just to the side of our trail. We greeted him innocently. Yes, we had crossed his fence. Yes, we were trespassing. We were just passing through. From his appearance, the farmer had come to the top of his farm to check out where he would hunt in a few weeks when deer season would begin. He had his rifle in hand. He looked us up and down. Then he stepped toward me, as I was in the lead on this shortcut to Spruce Falls.

"Who are you?" he demanded.

"I'm Greenbrier Almond, Doc Almond's son."

Suddenly he was enraged. His jaw set. His teeth clenched. He squinted and furrowed his brow. "I should have known!" he exploded. "I should shoot you dead!" he spoke through a tight lip, now very red in his face with arteries expanded in his neck and up the side of his face. Then he aimed his rifle at me and cocked it. From reading Jack London books of the Yukon Gold Rush, I could tell my life was in danger. I stepped back and lifted my right hand, forming the Boy Scout sign.

"Scout's Honor, we mean no harm. Let us pass."

An eternity of time passed, but at last he raised his gun and waved it in the air. "Get off my property. Don't ever come back!" he ordered. Indeed, we scurried double time over the hill and headed straight for Dr. Page's farmhouse. All of us vowed, that very minute, never to take a shortcut again!!!

Later, safe at home, I asked Dad what the rage was all about. He explained that Charlie Beer and he had been deer hunting on Dr. Page's farm, which adjoined this farmer's land. The deer were plentiful and jumping around. Dad spotted a 10-point buck with a wide spread of antlers. As he was taking aim, the trophy deer began to run. Dad fired as the deer was clearing the boundary fence. He hit it squarely so it fell dead as it hit the ground. Dad recalled, "I climbed the fence to get my deer when, just as today, the farmer stepped out from behind a tree and ordered me to stop. He said the deer was his." Charlie then stepped out from behind his tree and aimed his gun at the farmer. Dramatically, Charlie ordered Dad, "Go get your deer, Doc!" And Dad did.

"And what a fine deer it was," Dad recalled, wiping the sweat from his brow as he relived his own experience. "It was a deer to die for."

UPSHUR MOUNTAIN
SIGNPOSTS TO THE WORLD

World War II took a terrible toll on my parents. Dad lost his brother, and he himself spent eight years in the Army Air Corps. Mom saw drastic changes in her half-brothers. Both lost dear friends and grieved with those left behind. So when the five little Almonds wanted to take exotic vacations to far away places, Dad would just shake his head and simply say, "I've seen the world!" Mom remained curious to really know the people from Africa, the Middle East, Europe, South America, and Asia, so she opened our home to exchange students. Some came for a summer, some for a semester, some for a school year. Friday Neuko from Nigeria, Africa, stayed four years. With our well-rounded background, we curious children wondered just how far we were from the capitals of the world's nations. My 4-H talk on the "Seven Natural Wonders of Upshur County" gave us a chance to find the answer.

Upshur Mountain made our eminent list of natural wonders since, at 3053 feet, it is our tallest peak. The forest cover is great in southern Upshur County. Upshur Mountain stands like a green island rising out of a vast green sea, stretching 15 to 20 miles in all directions. On a West Virginia road map, it is unique in being located where there are no official roads. Driving out of Buckhannon at 1,400 feet above sea level, the climb is steady, winding through Tallmansville, Queens, Hemlock, High Germany, and finally to Upshur Mountain at the headwaters of the Middle Fork of the Tygart Valley River.

To further mark our isolation from the outside world, Mom and Dad helped K, Anne, Ruth, Beth, and me make signs labeling the distance from Upshur Mountain to the world's capitals: 3800 miles to London; 6706 miles to Tokyo; 9607 miles to Sydney; 5263 miles to Buenos Aires; 3971 miles to Paris; 8515 miles to Manila, for example.

With dozens of signs carefully painted, we carried our political science and geography lesson up the steep grade from where we parked our little green Jeep in a gurgling mountain stream. The trail wound through a cow pasture where the big-eyed Jerseys looked at this strange parade of explorers, then back into a deep forest, capping the final 500 feet of mossy and rocky soil to the top of Upshur Mountain.

Dad had me use my compass to mark north, south, east, and west so we could point our signs in the desired direction. Carefully with hammer and nails we began hanging signs on hardwood trees that had been growing for 80 years without such a commotion. How proud we were when all our signs were hung. Now anyone coming by Upshur Mountain who might be a stranger in these parts would know for certain the way to get to the bright lights and the enchanting music of places which we would continue only to imagine.

BIG FALLS ON
THE BUCKHANNON RIVER
"The Heart of Upshur County"

The "Seven Natural Wonders of Upshur County" grew out of a 4-H Public Speaking and Demonstration contest. After giving my talk to the local Upshurite 4-H Club, I presented at the county level, then at the regional at Jackson's Mill State 4-H Camp. For a basically shy guy, this was a big ordeal, but Dad and Mom, as well as my sisters, loved all the field trips to the various wonders. None was more fun than our picnic at the "Great Falls" on the Buckhannon River.

Always a doctor, Dad liked to personify Upshur County as a fictitious person, Judge Abel Parker Upshur. Buckhannon is his head, as it includes West Virginia Wesleyan College, the center for higher learning. The circulation system for "Judge Upshur" is comprised of our waterways. Our Buckhannon River is the great arterial vessel—the aorta. The division at Alexander is the right and left iliac/femoral arteries, with the right going on to the 4-H Camp at Selbyville and the left going on to Palace Valley and Upshur Mountain. But the heart of "Judge Upshur" is the "Great Falls" on the Buckhannon River. Just like a doctor auscultates the heart, listening to murmurs and to the rhythm, when we would arrive at the "Great Falls" near Ten Mile, we would expect to hear the rapids and feel the pulse and rhythm of our river as it tumbles over the sandstone ledge. To complete our exam, the Almond clan would plunge right into the river and shoot the rapids on our inner tubes. What a day of wonder and expectation!

More questions came from Doc as we rode along in the green Jeep, Mom riding shotgun and the rest of us piled in the back.

"How many miles to Ten Mile?"

"Ten."

"Who is buried in Grant's Tomb?"

"Grant."

"When is the Fourth of July celebrated?"

"The fourth of July."

The Almond clan could joke about anything. As we laughed our way to "Big Falls," we also got our prerequisite history lesson from Dad. Chief Buckongehanon of the mighty Delaware Indian tribe hunted these parts. Another day, we would all go to Indian Camp further upstream. His son, Mohanegon, died when ambushed on Lick Run by early settlers. The salt lick attracted deer and other animals, so it also attracted hunters wanting to feed their families. The young brave hid in waiting to shoot his bounty with a bow and arrow. But Captain White spotted him and mistakenly believed he was lying in ambush. He circled around the Indian and shot him in the back. The Indian Wars commenced. Bush's Fort was burned. The settlers who survived ran to West's Fort, now the town of Weston.

Soon we arrived high above the falls. Dad switched into four-wheel drive, and we headed down a steep grade under a giant overhanging rock ledge. Blackberries were ripe, so we hurried out of the Jeep and ate our way down the trail as Mom and Dad drove on. At the bottom, a large ballfield was carefully marked out. The sandy soil was bare of grass at home plate, first, second, and third bases. Local kids gathered on Sunday afternoons for play and for a reprieve from farm work. They probably headed for the "Great Falls" once they were hot and sweaty from a sandlot ball game.

Once again, memories were made, robust fun in the sun was had. We grew like Jesus who "increased in wisdom and stature, and in favour with God and man," as Mom, our 4-H leader, often recited from the official 4-H Bible verse, Luke 2:52.

WILDERNESS LEGACY
Independence Day 2011 Reflection

I am a kid again, anticipating the Almond Fourth of July picnic at the Wilderness, our family farm. The first of such picnics, I recollect, was when I was about eight years old. Mom and Dad did not actually purchase the Brain Farm until I was in 11th grade, but from the beginning we all loved picnicking and occasionally camping at the Wilderness in Hemlock, West Virginia.

The Fourth of July stands out as a special family holiday for several reasons:

* Dad insisted every holiday that the United States flag would fly in front of our home. On Independence Day, Old Glory flew throughout our patriotic mountain town.

* Mom looked for the date that watermelon dropped in price to a dollar per melon. This would usually be the 4th. So we tasted our first watermelon of the season. How we enjoyed spitting and shooting seeds, as well as slurping melon.

* West Virginia coal miners had the traditional Miner's Holiday the first two weeks in July. For many folks this included a trip to the beach, which was usually Myrtle Beach, South Carolina. So for Doc's practice, this meant a slowdown, with some extra time off for gardening and family time.

Over the years, the Fourth of July picnic trek proved a summer highlight at the Wilderness. Afternoon fun included sliding down the waterfalls, wearing out the bottoms of our cut-off jeans. Good and hungry, we relished picnic staples, including hot dogs and hamburgers. For dessert, we celebrated with s'mores over the evening campfire. We could not eat just one graham cracker sandwich with inside fixings of marshmallow melted in with Hershey chocolate. The cheer would be for some more! Some years we slept overnight, stargazing and listening for the whippoorwills.

K came up with the name "Wilderness." Later, she followed Grandfather and Grandmother Flanagan into the pastoral ministry. K practiced on us, having us read Scripture out loud around our campfire. One of her early sermons involved the calling of Jesus.

Of Jesus, Mark writes, "And immediately the spirit driveth him into the wilderness. And he was there in the wilderness 40 days, tempted of Satan; and was with the wild beasts; and the angels ministered unto him." (Mark 1:12,13)

The Spirit of joy has always been with us as we have gone to the Wilderness. For many years, we were driven in our little green Jeep. The summer between my 11th grade and 12th grade, I stayed 40 days in the Wilderness clearing brush. As Daddy Doc said, I had time to "cogitate." I had some help from local "angels," Cecil & Nellie Hoover, who lived about two miles away as the crow flies through the dense forest. They came over to help me "cut filth," as the brambles and briers were designated. The significance of my name, Greenbrier, was explained to me. Ol' timers called the greenbrier "rip shin," as it tore at the shins when a man strode through. Mr. Hoover explained that with a name like Greenbrier, I could stick to my goals and never let go, which would be positive, or I could rip shins, causing hurt and destruction to my environment or to my friends. The choice was mine. Which path would I follow?

I felt challenged and tempted. But in the end I took a path that grew me up into a stouthearted man, overcoming much. Now, I fear neither man nor beast. Such is the legacy of the Wilderness.

Also available

The Stories of a West Virginia Doctor
    Harold D. Almond, MD

Tender Loving Care: Stories of a West Virginia Doctor,
    Volume Two
        Stories of Harold Almond, MD as told to
        Greenbrier Almond, MD

Available from:
        McClain Printing Company
        1-800-654-7179
        http://www.mcclainprinting.com

        West Virginia Book Company
        1-888-982-7472
        http://www.wvbookco.com

        Amazon.com

        Barnesandnoble.com